Icons of Pop Music

Series Editors: Jill Halstead, Goldsmiths, University of London, and Dave Laing, independent writer and broadcaster

Books in this series, designed for undergraduates and the general reader, offer a critical profile of a key figure or group in twentieth-century pop music. These short paperback volumes focus on the work rather than on biography, and emphasize critical interpretation.

Published

The Velvet Underground
Richard Witts

Elvis Costello
Dai Griffiths

Forthcoming

Björk
Nicola Dibben

Elton John
Dave Laing

Joni Mitchell
Jill Halstead

BOB DYLAN

KEITH NEGUS

INDIANA
University Press
Bloomington & Indianapolis

921
DXLAN, B
NEGUS, K

3 1257 01781 3758

This book is a publication of

Indiana University Press
601 North Morton Street
Bloomington, Indiana 47404-3797, USA

http://iupress.indiana.edu

Telephone orders	800-842-6796
Fax orders	812-855-7931
Orders by e-mail	iuporder@indiana.edu

First published in the United Kingdom by Equinox Publishing Ltd.

Manufactured in Great Britain

Cataloging information is available from the Library of Congress.

ISBN   978-0-253-22005-9 (pbk.)

1 2 3 4 5 13 12 11 10 09 08

Contents

Acknowledgements

I am indebted to many people who have allowed me to try out ideas with them when discussing the music and songs of Bob Dylan. Special thanks to Chris Negus for countless conversations that have helped me clarify many of the ideas in this book. Special thanks too to Lee Marshall for numerous supportive dialogues, for forcing me to sort out my arguments, for spotting errors and inconsistencies in an early draft, and for supplying me with information and recordings. For comments and conversations that have also had a tangible impact upon this book, thanks to Rick Campion, Charlie Ford, Lucy Green, Dai Griffiths, Pete Astor, Simon Deacon, Jill Halstead, Catharine Mason, Rob Bowman, Mike Brocken, Mike Pickering and Patria Román-Velázquez. For his astute editing and encouragement throughout the project, thanks to Dave Laing. For their help throughout the entire process of publication and production, thanks to Sandra Margolies, Valerie Hall, Janet Joyce and Jane Behnken.

1 Surroundings

On 31 October 1964 Bob Dylan performed at the Philharmonic Hall in New York City, just two years after first signing a recording contract and with four albums already released. Having initially gained recognition as a folk "protest singer", he was rapidly moving away from songs of social commentary and "finger-pointing". Dylan was beginning to use the popular song in a new and radical manner to explore more internal or subjective experiences, whilst experimenting with the sound, meaning and rhythm of words. Within three months, when recording his fifth album, no longer performing alone with acoustic guitar and harmonica, he was creating an abrasive yet ethereal sonority, mixing the acoustic and electric textures of folk, electric blues, rock'n'roll, gospel, country and pop. The New York concert, which had been recorded for a planned live album, was no longer indicative of his music and its scheduled release was cancelled. Although it circulated amongst collectors, it was only released by Columbia Records nearly forty years later as *The Bootleg Series Vol. 6. Bob Dylan Live 1964. Concert At Philharmonic Hall.* Like other releases in the Bootleg series, the recording is a valuable document and provides a compelling insight into the way Dylan performed at the time.

Alone on stage with just an acoustic guitar and collection of harmonicas, Dylan creates an intimacy and immediacy of communication as he banters and jokes with fans throughout the performance. When he can't recall the opening lines of 'I Don't Believe You', his strumming stutters and he almost stops as he mumbles "Oh God". "Here's the second verse of it," he says before pausing and then asking the audience, "Does anybody know the first verse of this song?" A chorus of people yell out the opening line, and off he goes: "OK, this is the same song, it starts now." A number of times during the concert his guitar goes out of tune or he needs to change to a different tuning. Early in the concert he starts strumming the opening chords of 'If You Gotta Go, Go Now' and then halts to alter the pitch of his strings. As he's tuning he quips, "Don't let that scare you." Following a pause, during which he is adjusting the guitar, he then seemingly spontaneously says, "It's just Hallowe'en. I have my Bob Dylan mask on." The audience laugh knowingly, and then loudly applaud, as if they are colluding with him in their awareness of the stagecraft and characterization that have become integral to this "authentic" folk performer. "I'm masque-erading," he says in response and giggles.

On a concert recording made less than two years later, at Manchester Free Trade Hall on 17 May 1966, you can hear a very different dialogue with the audience (*The Bootleg Series Vol. 4. Bob Dylan Live 1966. The "Royal Albert Hall" Concert*). During the opening acoustic set of Dylan's show the audience had listened to familiar and new songs in reverential silence and responded with enthusiastic but polite applause. When he returned for the second half, a vocal section of the audience was clearly outraged at Dylan's decision to perform both old and new songs with a band of electric guitars, bass, drums and keyboards. At this concert there is no friendly banter prior to 'I Don't Believe You'. Instead, Dylan emphasizes how he's moved on from his folk days by casually drawling, "This is called 'I Don't Believe You' – it used to be like that and now it goes like this." A snap on the snare drum and a pulsating bass introduce the song. It has been raised a tone in pitch from D to E – the ringing metallic timbre of the E chord, using all six strings of the electric guitar, and the higher pitch of Dylan's vocal over the rhythms of the band accentuate the song's transformation from a slightly bemused, restrained acoustic folk lament about a lover who pretends they've never met to a defiant electric blues, the anger spilling over from the specific events described in the lyrics and expressing a more general sense of disaffection.

British folk fans, familiar with and expecting acoustic music, were hearing one of the noisiest of early amplified rock gigs. Many were clearly bewildered. Some became audibly angry and continued slow handclapping and shouting taunts at the stage – responses that had followed Dylan on this tour. Just before the final song the recording captures the infamous shout of "Judas!", followed by applause from a section of the audience. There is a pause and then Dylan retorts with the words that don't actually feature in the lyrics of the song despite its title: "I don't believe you." There is a further pause before he spits out, "You're a liar." The band cascades into 'Like A

Rolling Stone', the song that was then defining how anger and alienation could be expressed in rock music.

These recordings and the specific incidents give an insight into a captivating performer, rapidly undergoing creative changes. They also highlight the way Dylan has always been primarily a performing artist. When he began songwriting he had already been performing for several years, and the songs he started writing were created because he was dissatisfied with the limitations of his existing repertoire and wanted material that he could sing with conviction. Most of his early songs extended or developed some of the existing folk material that he had been playing in clubs and coffee-houses.

Dylan's songs have usually been written from a performer's perspective. In the early 1960s, they were tailored to his rhythmic strummed guitar style, his bohemian folksy persona and the nasal folk-blues voice of his early recordings and concerts. In later years, the songs would be written to be performed by changing bands of musicians and to accommodate Dylan's engagement with various blues, country, ballad, gospel, rock and pop styles. The songs would then be continually refined and developed during subsequent performances – changed in response to the musical styles inspiring Dylan at the time and changed in relation to the musicians available. The songs have also been reshaped over the years according to Dylan's decision to perform them on acoustic or electric guitar, or on acoustic or electric piano, or (on very rare occasions) when he has put aside his instrument and sung at the microphone in front of a band.

Unlike many of his artistic peers who achieved their initial critical acclaim and commercial success during the 1960s, Dylan did not "compose" his songs with recording in mind, nor did he spend hours in the studio perfecting his music as a recorded artefact (as the Beatles and the Beach Boys began to do). The songwriter Paul Zollo once asked him, "Until you record a song, no matter how heroic it is, it doesn't really exist. Do you ever feel that?" Dylan replied, "No. If it's there, it exists" (Zollo 2003: 79). This is a very different attitude from the belief that one recording can be selected from various studio versions and live performances and deemed a "definitive version" (Scobie 2003: 254), as if an "original" can be isolated as a kind of *urtext*. As Dylan later remarked, "A record is not that monumental for me to make. It's just a record of songs" (Rosenbaum 1978: 70). Most of Dylan's recordings are a document of his songs caught at a particular moment in the life of the song and its author. The songs as recorded are usually identifiable in concert, but changes may be made to lyrics, melody, rhythm, tempo and harmony. This is why performance has been so central to his life as a songwriter and this is why Paul Williams has argued that Dylan's "finest work has been done … outside of the confines of the recording studio" (1992: xiv).

The first officially released studio recording of a song is neither definitive nor authoritative. As Dylan observed in 1993: "The songs I recorded in my past, they're almost like demos. I'm still trying to figure out what some of them are about. The more I play them, the better idea I have of how to play them" (Muir 2001: 92). During the same year he added, "Time lets me find new meanings to every song, even in the older ones, and it's important to be always looking for new meanings. Yes, the body of the song remains the same but it wears new clothes" (Roe 2003: 90). Only very rarely have the new clothes included changes to lyrics; Dylan has found the new meanings in the music. You only have to listen to the New York version of 'I Don't Believe You' in October 1964 and the "same" song at Manchester in May 1966 to realize that the new clothes can provide revealing insights into Dylan's changing musical identity. His live performances have continually provoked audiences into thinking about the songs differently, sending listeners back to play the recordings again and to hear them in a new light.

The audience has always been part of Dylan's music as a tangible physical presence. From the fans who helped him remember the first line of 'I Don't Believe You' to the fan who felt disappointed enough to yell "Judas!" there is a long history of communication between Dylan and his audience. This has ranged between those who have voiced their disappointment and their disapproval to an almost ecstatic response – very often at the same concert. Fans have verbally objected or walked out in response to apocalyptic pronouncements inspired by self-righteous Christianity during the late 1970s or to the shambolic performances during the winter of 1991. Yet fans have roared their approval continually over the years. The good-natured banter between musician on stage and fans in the audience featured less after the early 1960s, but occasionally appeared during the mid-1990s. Dylan's concerts and performances on albums have continually inspired. Yet they have also offended, outraged and perturbed those listeners who assumed that they knew who Bob Dylan was, what he would sing about and what his music would sound like.

The mask and the musician

Writing about how he has confounded his followers, a number of commentators have picked up on Dylan's quip about wearing the Bob Dylan mask. Rather than a light-hearted, flippant or ironic remark, it has been taken as an insight into Dylan's art and performing identity.

Stephen Scobie draws parallels with the way players in Greek and Roman theatre used masks "to conceal identity and to express character" (2003: 46). Just as this enabled one actor to assume many roles, so too Dylan's mask of performance "multiplies identity" and allowed "identity itself to become an artistic construct" (*ibid.*: 47). Scobie stresses how the English term "person" has evolved from the Latin *persona* and, referring to the writings of poet Ezra Pound, declares:

> There has always been an element of the Poundian *persona* in Dylan's work. In a strictly limited sense, a *persona* is an adopted voice: a poem in which the poet, though writing in the first person, is manifestly taking on the role of a fictional character. (*ibid.*: 48)

He goes on to give examples in the poetry of Robert Browning and T. S. Eliot and argues that when Dylan sings "I" in a song it is "always, as a *persona*, as a mask" (*ibid.*). Scobie cites Rimbaud's "I is another", a phrase used by other critics when writing about the persona of Bob Dylan, and one which Dylan has also rather mischievously quoted back at them (see Crowe 1985; Day 1988), particularly when trying to deflect autobiographical interpretations of his work.

For Scobie, Dylan's creativity cannot be narrowly located in his lyrics and music without acknowledging the parallel production of an idiosyncratic performing identity. It is not only his songs that have been creatively rearranged over time, so too has the appearance and manner of the singer. Scobie writes of what he calls "the mask of originality" (2003: 48), pointing to how Dylan has adopted various personas, continually creating and discarding "masks of himself" such as the "protest singer, rock star and country gentleman" (*ibid.*). Scobie locates Dylan "within the carnivalesque tradition of acting and masking" (*ibid.*: 49), his identity always in doubt, always out of reach and forever confounding the critical interpreter.

This is a vision of artistic identity refracted through drama, spectacle, poetry and fiction into popular music. It resonates with the idea that an artist creates a self simultaneously with his or her art and links the literary aesthetic of romantic poets and novelists to modern pop culture. One of its legacies is the now almost commonplace assumption that pop musicians are invented characters, continually subject to change as they are subsequently "reinvented" – an idea that frames both the critical interpretation and commercial marketing of numerous artists, including David Bowie, Madonna, Prince and Bruce Springsteen.

Dylan's awareness of the mask or persona, and the labour that goes with it, was seemingly signalled at a press conference during the 1980s when he said, "I'm only Bob Dylan when I have to be". When asked who he was the rest of the time, he replied "myself" (Heylin 2000: 4). For a famous musician to say such a thing – whether earnestly or flippantly – is not unusual. Many performers from across a range of music genres have made similar comments, aware of the need to create a distinction or a space between their public appearance and a more private sense of the self. It is one of the practical ways of coping with fame, a strategy for dealing with false information that may be circulated in the media. At one point in the documentary film of his 1965 tour of Britain, *Don't Look Back*, Dylan is seen reading about himself in a newspaper and declaring "I'm glad that I'm not me" – realizing that the public's knowledge of Bob Dylan is also created by the ideas and misrepresentations of others and not at all controlled by the masked man. To say "I'm only Bob Dylan when I have to be" is also an acknowledgement of how performers have to be an "act" when they step out on stage or into the public realm.

It is the identity and music of this public act that concerns Lee Marshall in his study of Dylan's stardom. Adopting a sociological perspective, in contrast to Scobie's literary or poetic approach, Marshall is concerned with Dylan as a "star-image" and is more emphatic about the futility of seeking a "real", "authentic" or "true" man behind the mask. For Marshall neither biographical investigations nor lyrical detective work will reveal a concealed creator, because there is no hidden musician lurking behind the words and images. Dylan appears before us – singing, speaking, playing an instrument, writing words on a page, introducing a record on the radio. As Marshall puts it,

> What you see is what there is and, while what we see may
> suggest to us a reality to which we do not have access, and
> while we may like to believe that there is something there,
> in the end, what we see is all there is. (2007: 38)

The biographer who wishes to get behind the "star-image", or the critic
who wishes to dislodge the performer's mask and so glimpse the "naked"
or "true face" (Marcus, 1997), will still be, paradoxically, contributing to
Dylan's star-image. Whilst I'm not quite as confident as Marshall in believing
that "there is no time when Bob Dylan isn't 'Bob Dylan'" (2007: 40), what
finally comes over forcefully from Marshall's sociological reflections on Dylan's
stardom is strikingly obvious yet extremely insightful:

> As fans and critics, we spend a lot of time and energy
> searching for the "real" Bob Dylan. We already know the real
> Bob Dylan, however: it is the one we hear on record, see on
> stage, read in interviews. Whatever we think, know or believe
> about Dylan, we think, know or believe *from what we see in
> front of us*, not from anything backstage. (*ibid.*: 41)

The music that has inspired and fascinated me has come from the Bob
Dylan that has appeared in front of us – listeners, audiences, fans – reaching
out to us from recordings, radios, stages, screens and words on a page. In
front of us, most of the time, is Bob Dylan the musician, making music,
talking about music, writing about music, even playing the part of a musician
in most of his film roles. Most writings about Dylan, however, have tended
to ignore his musicianship and the musical characteristics of his songs,
focusing instead on lyrics and life story. I'm interested in Dylan's songs as
music that is performed rather than written poetry (I'm not denying the
importance of the words or the life story and I have drawn valuable ideas
from biographies and studies of Dylan's lyrics). When Dylan's performances
have been discussed, the emphasis has frequently been on the performance
of a persona or character, rather than the performance of a musician. I hope
this book will begin to correct the view that there is little to say about the
music – an assumption often implied, and only occasionally stated explicitly,
in much writing about Dylan. In fact, there is much more to be said about
Dylan's music and musicianship than I've been able to include in this book.

In dwelling on what I think is a neglected aspect of Dylan's creativity, I've drawn upon and emphasized certain biographical details that give an insight into how his artistic sensibility was formed. In this chapter, in particular, I've homed in on the circumstances that shaped him and the contexts, experiences and surroundings that allowed him to pursue a musician's life and create himself as Bob Dylan the performer and songwriter.

Home and family

The boy who would become the musician was born in Duluth, Minnesota, on 24 May 1941, and named Robert Allen Zimmerman. He began using the stage name Bob Dylan after a series of reflections, sometime in the latter part of 1959, about how he should present himself as a performer. Like any number of musicians, actors and actresses, and to a slightly lesser degree novelists and painters, Robert Zimmerman adopted a pseudonym with the aim of signalling himself as an artist with a distinct identity. From his mid-teens Bobby Zimmerman had been putting considerable effort and time into creating what would become his Bob Dylan identity. He worked on his voice, his gestures, his guitar and piano-playing technique, his hairstyle and clothing, his autobiography (the fictitious stories he would tell about his life) and, of course, his music and rhythms, lyrics and rhymes.

Before he adopted the name Bob Dylan he called himself Elston Gunn when playing piano and singing in a rock'n'roll band. When seeking a name he'd also considered dropping his surname and calling himself Robert Allen. But it was "Dylan" that encapsulated the identity he wished to present. As he recalls in *Chronicles: Volume One* (2004), he spent some time thinking about how different names would sound when spoken and how they would look in print (spelt, for example, as Dillon). Not only did this stage name reference the poet Dylan Thomas, regardless of whether he'd read the poetry (not very pop or rock'n'roll in 1959), it was blunt Bob, not the softer Bobby, that was preferred.

These name changes were, as Marshall (2007) emphasizes, steps on a route towards stardom, and the search for a name stopped with Bob Dylan. It sounded good when spoken. It looked good when written. It had a certain "star" quality. The choice of surname – Dylan – was very different from the Jewish Zimmerman and has sometimes been construed as a denial of his background. This point is taken up by Michael Billig when discussing how Dylan and other musicians of his generation dropped their Jewish surnames:

> For many Jews these changes of surname were no big deal. They were not breaking centuries of family tradition. Most of the surnames, in any case, had been acquired in the last hundred years, often imposed by the state authorities in Eastern Europe ... Robert Zimmerman might have been taking a predictable step when he emerged as Bob Dylan, but his parents had already helped him on the way. They had given him easily assimilable forenames: Robert Allen. He was not saddled, in the Christian north-west, with Isaac, Irving, or indeed, Abraham, like his father. (2000: 121)

Dylan was also aware of how members of his family, like many other immigrants to the United States, had changed their names to avoid prejudice and to become less conspicuous when *becoming* Americans. His Lithuanian maternal grandfather Benjamin did so when he changed his name from Solemovitz to Stone.

Many families in the United States in the first half of the twentieth century had first-hand experience of migration and immigration to the New World. Bob's father was Abe (Abram) Zimmerman, the son of Zigman and Anna Zimmerman, Jews who had fled from the port of Odessa in Ukraine when anti-Semitic persecution escalated during the early years of the twentieth century. Like so many immigrants, Bob's paternal grandfather Zigman "gravitated to a place similar to the land where he was born" (Sounes 2001: 31). Duluth was a busy port like Odessa and had a similar climate, characterized by short summers and long cold winters. Bob's grandparents came to the United States with three children, and a further three (including Bob's father Abram) were born in Duluth. Bob's mother, Beatty (Beatrice) Stone, was from Hibbing, north of Duluth, a town to which the family would move when Bob was five years old. Her maternal grandparents were Jewish émigrés from Lithuania. Bob had a younger brother David, and some accounts have suggested that they were not particularly close as children (in order to emphasize the apparently solitary and detached quality of Bob's character). Throughout his life as a public figure, Dylan has understandably guarded his privacy. Although the two brothers are reported to have engaged in some shared business interests, little is known publicly of their sibling relationship. What we do know suggests that they are probably quite close. Close enough for Bob to trust David with a significant role in organizing the studio sessions in Minneapolis that produced a number of the recordings that feature on *Blood On The Tracks* (Gill and Odegard 2004).

From his earliest years Robert Zimmerman became aware of the significance and experience of being Jewish, of being connected with the Old World within the New World. Initially, as he grew up, there were family stories that he heard from his parents and grandparents. For a few summers in his early teens he attended the Zionist summer camps run by the Hadassah Club (Shelton 1986: 45). At thirteen he undertook the formal ritual of the bar mitzvah, which involves the public reading of the Torah in a synagogue. In preparation he studied Hebrew with a rabbi and he delivered the reading as a form of ritualistic chant known as cantillation. His parents remembered that about four hundred people attended Bob's bar mitzvah (*ibid.*: 36). In later life he would attend the bar mitzvahs for his own sons and he occasionally acknowledged publicly an interest in the influence of his Jewish background and, perhaps inevitably, an awareness of anti-Semitism. Clinton Heylin quotes him as saying, "I'm interested in what and who a Jew is, I'm interested in the fact that Jews are Semites, like Babylonians, Hittites, Arabs, Syrians, Ethiopians. But a Jew is different because a lot of people hate Jews" (2000: 329).

During a visit to Israel in 1971 he was asked why he didn't make a public declaration about his Jewish identity. He replied, "There is no problem. I'm a Jew. It touches my poetry, my life, in ways I can't describe. Why should I declare something that should be so obvious?" (Shelton 1986: 413). The influence is indeed obvious in Dylan's song lyrics, and many writers have referred to the way he has drawn extensively on the Old Testament. The Jewish influence seems far less obvious when it comes to his music. In one of the few reflections on this point, Wilfrid Mellers picked up on a comment in the liner notes for *Desire* where Allen Ginsberg had written of Dylan's voice in 'One More Cup Of Coffee' as "Hebraic cantillation never before heard in U.S. song" (Ginsberg 1976: 21). From this, Mellers later speculated on the Jewish influence in Dylan's music:

> ... although there is little direct musical evidence of his
> Jewish ancestry, the nasally inflected, melismatic style of
> cantillation found in extreme form in 'One More Cup Of
> Coffee' is more pervasive than might at first be suspected.
> Particularly in the songs concerned with the landscape and
> mythology of the Wild West and of the Texan, Arizonan and
> New Mexican deserts, Dylan's singing may rediscover age-old
> links between the Hebraic, the Moorish and the Spanish, and
> may also reveal affinities with the starker musics of the Red
> Indians themselves. (1984: 221)

Mellers's inferences are intriguing, but Dylan's vocal performance in 'One More Cup Of Coffee' is untypical and, apart from a few vocal slides on some of the other tracks on *Desire*, it is not easy to find "pervasive" examples of these musical influences across Dylan's work as a whole.

In the early 1980s Dylan was again reported to be engaging with aspects of his Jewish background. The cover art for the album *Infidels* featured imagery of Jerusalem, although there was little evidence of Jewish sounds, the music being a rather bland blend of bluesy rock and light reggae. During his 1984 summer concert tour he observed the Jewish Sabbath by not giving concerts on Fridays and Saturdays (Cartwright 1993: 122). In 1983 he responded to an interviewer's question about his "so-called Jewish roots" in the following way:

> "Roots man – we're talking about Jewish roots, you want to
> know more? Check upon Elijah the prophet. He could make
> rain. Isaiah the prophet, even Jeremiah, see if their brethren
> didn't want to bust their brains for telling it right like it is,
> yeah – these are my roots I suppose. Am I looking for them?
> Well, I don't know. I ain't looking for them in synagogues with
> six pointed Egyptian stars shining down from every window,
> I can tell you that much." (*ibid.*)

Although the Zimmerman family observed the Jewish religion and were acutely aware of their background, like most immigrants to the United States they were actively encouraged to assimilate to an "American" way of life. Robert became aware of being part of something much larger, a diasporic people with a history of having no identifiable homeland. But he was born in the United States and the transnational character of these Jewish ties was vague and abstract rather than a tangible part of everyday life. He grew up in a small place, at a slow pace. It was slightly detached, removed from the immediate traumas of World War II, and away from the pace and density of life in the cities. In *Chronicles: Volume One* Dylan recalled the games he played as a child in the country and remarked, "With not much media to speak of, it was basically life as you saw it" (2004: 232).

Robert Zimmerman grew up in a comfortable and supportive middle-class home. His father worked in management at Standard Oil until he contracted polio. After recuperating he went into partnership with his brothers at the Micka Electric retail store. Whilst biographers have sometimes picked up on ways that Dylan's relationship with his father was occasionally strained (perhaps a generational commonplace at the time, and something that biographers of a rock musician might wish to emphasize), in his early teens he wrote sensitive poems that he presented to Abram on Father's Day. Abe died in June 1968, when Dylan was twenty-seven.

Bob also wrote touching poems that he gave to Beatty for Mother's Day (Shelton 1986). He was close to his mother throughout her life until her death in January 2000, when audiences noticed a marked sombreness as he took to the stage dressed in black. This closeness was visible when his mother appeared on stage with him during the Rolling Thunder Revue tour in 1975 and she was regularly part of his entourage during the 1980s. According to the limited information available, Bob has continued to maintain close ties with his own children and grandchildren.

Words, sounds and dreams

The poems that Bob wrote for and gave to his parents were indications of a growing interest in literature and poetry. During the 1960s his mother told biographer Robert Shelton of how he would shut himself away in his room, remembering

> "Bob was upstairs quietly becoming a writer for twelve years. He read every book there was ... I said to Bobby that you can't go on and on and on and sit and dream and write poems. I was afraid he would end up being a poet! Do you know the kind of poet I mean? One that had no ambition and wrote only for himself." (Shelton 1986: 41–2)

Howard Sounes, like a number of commentators, has characterized Bob as "a solitary, contemplative child" (2001: 40). This solitary and contemplative character was clearly an asset in developing his musical and literary sensibility; poets and musicians tend to have spent considerable time alone thinking about, practising and perfecting their craft. When Shelton spoke with Bob's mother, she stressed that "He was never detached from family and friends, but he dreamt a lot" (1986: 41). Dylan has often spoken and written of the way he daydreamed as a child. In an interview he recalled:

> "I had some amazing projections when I was a kid, but not since then. And those visions have been strong enough to keep me going today. ... I was born in, grew up in a place so foreign that you had to be there to picture it. ... in the winter, everything was still, nothing moved. Eight months of that. You can put it together. You can have some amazing hallucinogenic experiences doing nothing but looking out your window. There is also the summer, when it gets hot and sticky and the air is very metallic. There is a lot of Indian spirit. The earth there is unusual, filled with ore. So there is something happening that is hard to define." (Rosenbaum 1978: 62)

Dylan's comments about his dreams and imaginings indicate that his sensibilities were influenced by the physical or material texture of the world that he was growing up in: the way it felt (hot, cold, sticky); the pace of life (nothing moving); the ambience of the ground and landscape (the earth). The weather – that unavoidable part of our environment that can have such an impact on our mood – is forever present in Dylan's lyrics as rain, wind, storms, clouds, sky, thunder and lightning. As he told an interviewer, "Environment affects me a great deal ... A lot of the songs [on *Time Out Of Mind*] were written after the sun went down. And I like storms, I like to stay up during a storm. I get very meditative sometimes" (Pareles 1997).

This sensitivity to surroundings and the imaginings they provoked clearly shaped his artistic sensibility. Sounes evokes the ambience surrounding the young child – the sights, the smells and the sounds:

> The central hillside district of Duluth was predominantly Jewish and Polish, with a synagogue at the end of the road. There was a general store, a European bakery, the Loiselle

liquor store, and a Sears Roebuck at the bottom of the hill. The weather was determined by Lake Superior, so vast and deep it remained icy cold throughout the year. Even in mid-summer, Duluth could be shrouded in frigid fog. There was a fresh ocean smell and the cry of seagulls. Ships approaching the landmark Ariel Bridge sounded their horns and a horn on the bridge blasted in reply. These were the sights and sounds that Bob grew up with as the Second World War raged to its end. (2001: 34)

In *Chronicles: Volume One* Dylan evocatively recalled this environment and its impact on his senses – the material, physical presence of sound, engulfing him and resonating within his body:

What I recall mostly about Duluth are the slate gray skies and the mysterious foghorns, violent storms that always seemed to be coming straight at you and merciless howling winds off the big black mysterious lake with treacherous ten-foot waves … Ships from South America, Asia and Europe came and went all the time, and the heavy rumble of foghorns dragged you out of your senses by the neck. Even though you couldn't see the ships through the fog, you knew they were there by the heavy outbursts of thunder that blasted like Beethoven's Fifth – two low notes, the first one long and deep like a bassoon. Foghorns sounded like great announcements. The big boats came and went, iron monsters from the deep – ships to wipe out all spectacles. As a child, slight, introverted and asthma stricken, the sound was so loud, so enveloping, I could feel it in my whole body and it made me feel hollow. Something out there could swallow me up. (2004: 230, 273–4)

Sound is very important in early life. The unborn baby initially orients itself to the sounds in its environment and the rhythms of the mother's body (DeNora 2000). When we are born, before we can focus our eyes on any visible object, we become conscious of a world of sound. We quickly learn to recognize the sound of pleasure, of pain, of joy, of anxiety. We soon realize how the sounds we make have a physical impact on those around us. The baby's cry is not simply a pre-verbal message. The young child's scream has a material, physical impact – it sets the air vibrating. If you are close enough, you will physically feel it.

The term "soundscape" was introduced by R. Murray Schafer (1993) to indicate how the sonic environment influences our perception and knowledge. He coined the term "soundmark" (from landmark) to emphasize how "keynote sounds of a landscape" can imprint "themselves so deeply on people hearing them" (1994: 10). Philip Tagg (1994) has developed this theme in a number of writings, covering music from Mozart to hip-hop, sounds from animals to motorbikes, places from twentieth-century India to medieval Europe. His point is that the sounds which surround us influence the music we make and listen to, shaping how we understand the world we inhabit.

Like many composers, songwriters and performers, Bob Dylan has always been acutely aware of the sound and the texture of his surroundings. Shelton quotes a friend Sybil Weinberger: "He was so aware of his surroundings, in every situation, it was almost like he couldn't write fast enough. Dylan would get thoughts and reactions and he would stop on a street corner and write things down" (1986: 136). Dylan himself has recalled how, when he first came to New York City, he found the sound of trains comforting:

> I'd seen and heard trains from my earliest childhood days and the sight and sound of them always made me feel secure. The big boxcars, the iron ore cars, freight cars, passenger trains, Pullman cars. There was no place you could go in my home-town without at least some part of the day having to stop at intersections and wait for the long trains to pass … The sound of trains off in the distance more or less made me feel at home, like nothing was missing … The ringing of bells made me feel at home, too. (2004: 31)

In his reflections on the impact of the "sonic environment" Schafer has written more generally of how trains have imparted a repertoire of rhythms, pitches and timbres into human life – the chuffing engine, the escaping steam, the rattling of coaches, the clatter of tracks, the squeaking of wheels (1994: 81).

Like a number of writers, Albert Murray has referred to the extensive railroad imagery in blues titles and lyrics and has written about how the sound of the blues has been influenced by trains. Of the significance of the "heroic beat" of steam trains with their bells and whistles, he writes:

> The influence of the old smoke-chugging railroad-train engine on the sound of blues music may or may not have been as great as that of the downhome church, but both have been definitive, and sometimes it's hard to say which is the source of what ... one call-and-response sequence may have derived directly from the solo call of the minister and the ensemble response of the congregation in the church service; but another ... may well have come from the solo call of the train whistle and the ensemble response of the pumping pistons and rumbling boxcars ... some of the great variety of bell-like piano sounds that so many blues musicians, piano players in particular, like to play around with may sometimes be stylizations of church bells ringing for Sunday Morning Service, sending tidings, tolling for the dead, and so on; but most often they seem to be train bells. (Murray 2000: 124)

Murray notes the way cymbals can evoke the percussive effect of "locomotive steam", and points to the more obvious impact of train whistles on guitar and harmonica styles. Others have written of how chugging train rhythms have influenced blues guitar styles. Paul Oliver has noted how railroad workers would arrange the steam whistles on trains so that they would play a basic tune: "On the Illinois Central, the famous IC which ran from Chicago to New Orleans, the firemen would send a rudimentary blues wailing across the Delta by 'quilling' on the whistles" (1990: 64). Murray, and to a lesser extent Oliver, have evoked the subtle ways that the sounds of the environment become part of a musical style and its craft conventions, informing the sensibilities and sonic palette of musicians.

The percussive blues pattern, the locomotive rhythm and the imagery of trains, also present in country music, continued to be an integral strand of mainstream popular music during the latter part of the twentieth century, running from Elvis Presley's rendition of 'Mystery Train' in 1956 to Kraftwerk's 'Trans-Europe Express' in 1977, from David Bowie's 'Station To Station' in 1976 to OutKast's 'The Train' in 2006. The imagery and the sound of trains has always been an integral part of Bob Dylan's music, absorbed both directly and through the blues. It was particularly present during the 1960s, right from the "steadily building locomotive rhythms on the guitar thrust up against exquisitely sustained train whistle vocalizations" (Williams 1990: 67) on 'Rocks And Gravel' performed in 1962 through to the railroad, engine and train imagery and more subtle use of locomotive rhythms and metallic timbres that Dylan transmuted into the textures of *Highway 61 Revisited* and *Blonde On Blonde*.

Dylan has quite consciously thought of his music in relation to the sonic textures of the environment, with trains and bells featuring in how he hears his sound. On one of the few occasions when an interviewer has asked him about this, he reflected:

> "The closest I ever got to the sound I hear in my mind was on individual bands in the *Blonde on Blonde* album. It's that thin, that wild mercury sound. It's metallic and bright gold, with whatever that conjures up. That's my particular sound. I haven't been able to succeed in getting it all the time. Mostly, I've been driving at a combination of guitar, harmonica and organ, but now I find myself going into territory that has more percussion in it and rhythms of the soul ... It was the sound of the streets ... That ethereal twilight light, you know. It's the sound of the street with the sunrays, the sun shining down at a particular time, on a particular type of building. A particular type of people walking on a particular type of street. It's an outdoor sound that drifts even into open windows that you can hear. The sound of bells and distant railroad trains and arguments in apartments and the clinking of silverware and knives and forks and beating with leather straps. It's all – it's all there ... no jackhammer sounds, no airplane sounds ... water trickling down a brook. It's light flowing through the ... [interruption by interviewer] ... crack of dawn ... music filters out to me in the crack of dawn." (Rosenbaum 1978: 69–70)

Again, in this quote, Dylan is bodily attuned to the texture of his surroundings and its sounds becoming music. It is a specific mixture of sounds that he wants to incorporate – bells, distant railroad trains, trickling water, but not airplanes. And he attempts to convey the way it filters to him as music at the crack of dawn, a moment when the body may be coming out of dreams or when we can allow the mind to freeplay in a semi-dreamlike state.

A different set of dreams, soundtracks and environments was available to the young Bobby Zimmerman through the growing mass media of radio, television, records and movies. Experimental broadcasts had begun in the USA in the late 1930s, but television only started to become a widely used domestic medium from the early 1950s. The Zimmerman family had a television set in 1952 and, although broadcasts were infrequent and reception often poor, the small screen brought the sounds and images of musicians directly into the home. Elvis Presley and Hank Williams appeared, along with a world of escape into Westerns, science fiction and slapstick.

Like so many young people growing up in the United States during the 1950s, Bobby Zimmerman dreamed himself home from the cinema after seeing the romantic, rebellious, misunderstood characters portrayed by the vulnerable James Dean and the defiant, leather-clad Marlon Brando (Shelton 1986). The exaggerated idiosyncratic movements of Charlie Chaplin's caring and dishevelled tramp also had a formative influence on his approach to performance. Dylan told Shelton, "He influences me, even in the way I sing. His films really sank in" (*ibid.*: 125). In New York during 1961 Dylan would often tell rambling, formless, open-ended, stream-of-consciousness, shaggy dog stories in between songs. His audiences found them funny, often responding more to "his wit than to his slow, serious, intense material. Audience reaction led him to play Chaplinesque clown" (*ibid.*: 109).

Radio had been introduced during the 1920s, and Dylan was, in his own words, "always fishing for something on the radio. Just like trains and bells, it was part of the soundtrack of my life" (2004: 32). Bobby Zimmerman turned his radio dial at night and stayed listening to the early hours of the morning, tuning in to broadcasts of recordings by blues singers such as Howlin' Wolf and Muddy Waters, country singers such as Hank Williams and the Carter Family, crooners such as Frank Sinatra. Dylan acknowledged his debt to and love of radio when he became a softly spoken DJ and hosted a series of Theme Time Radio Hours throughout 2006 and 2007. Although the young Bobby Zimmerman went to concerts, attending one of the last performances by Buddy Holly, it was radio and records that inspired him to want to make music of his own.

Becoming a musician

Bob did not grow up in an overtly musical family, although his father had played the violin when he was a younger man and his mother could play the piano. The family house contained a baby grand piano, and Abe and Beatty encouraged their sons to develop an interest in music. When Bob was about eleven years old he was given a few piano lessons by a cousin. While his brother David persevered with formal tuition, Bob taught himself to play the piano from listening, experiment and observation. Typically for a self-taught pianist with a love of rock'n'roll and blues, and for whom Little Richard was a particular hero, Bob developed a highly rhythmic style of piano-playing. He once recalled, "I used to play piano like Little Richard style. Only I used to play, you know, an octave higher, and everything came out … His mistake was he played down too low … I played everything high, and it amplified" (Williams 1990: 38).

Whereas classically trained pianists are taught to emphasize melodies that cover wide pitch ranges and to explore numerous chords and scales, in blues, rock'n'roll and rock music the piano is often far more significant for its contribution to rhythm and for the way it may support singers or instrumentalists with rhythmic vamping or riffing (in contrast to the noodlings of classically trained pop and jazz pianists). Although some audience members were surprised when Dylan began playing electric piano on stage during October 2002, the piano had been the instrument he played most frequently during his early years as a musician. One of the first groups he formed with two friends was a vocal trio called the Jokers. Sounes reports that they performed "wherever they could find a piano, including high school dances" (2001: 48). They also performed on a local television talent show and in the summer of 1956 they paid to make a 78-rpm recording of 'Be-Bop-A-Lula' and 'Earth Angel'. One of Bob's first girlfriends, Echo Star Helstrom, recalled that "he could play the piano like an old blues guy" (ibid.: 53).

Bob tinkered around with both saxophone and trumpet before teaching himself to play acoustic guitar. Like so many popular musicians, he had no formal musical tuition. He learnt from the basic advice about chord shapes, picking and strumming given in do-it-yourself guides and by listening to recordings, observing other musicians, heeding their advice, experimenting alone, and from endlessly talking with friends and musicians about music. As a teenager Bob developed a skill that is vital for musicians who do not

© Brian Shuel/Redferns

In London 1962

perform by "reading" notation – the ability to listen intently and to absorb and acquire melodies, chords and rhythms through the ear (rather than by interpreting a schematic representation of music with the eye). Throughout Dylan's life many musicians who have performed with him have commented upon his ability to grasp songs very quickly and to absorb music from his surroundings. The term "sponge" features in many comments. The singer Liam Clancy is not the only person to have likened Dylan during his early years as a performer to "blotting paper. He soaked everything up. He had this immense curiosity" (1987: 21). Folk musician Martin Carthy used the same analogy: "Bob Dylan's a piece of blotting paper when it comes to listening to tunes. If he doesn't learn the tune, he learns the idea of the tune and he can do something like it" (Heylin 2000: 106).

Dylan also developed the ability to transpose a song almost instantly, that is, to change the key of a song without having to think too much about it. Changing key most obviously means that a singer pitches his or her voice higher or lower, with the vocal chords tensing, straining or relaxing and so affecting the timbre of the voice. A change of key may also suggest different melodic shapes in the same register, and imply different fingerings on the guitar. It generates various aesthetic decisions concerning melody, chord and timbre; some keys will allow more open, ringing chords that use all six strings (E or A), or chords can be played on three strings to create a softer or stabbing effect. Like other folk and blues guitarists, Dylan experimented with different guitar tunings. In the early 1960s he often used "dropped" tunings, lowering the pitch of the bottom string from an E to a D or a C, giving an extended and deeper bass resonance.

Not long after the Jokers, Bob became leader and played piano with the Shadow Blasters. Very much influenced by Little Richard, at one of their shows in a school auditorium they took to the stage dressed in pink shirts, dark glasses, and with hair brushed into quiffs. Although Bob strolled around Hibbing with an acoustic guitar slung over his shoulder, and even acquired a cheap electric guitar, he continued to play piano in bands and eventually formed a trio of guitar, drums and piano billed as Bobby Zimmerman and the Golden Chords. In 1958 he played with this band, standing at the piano, moving backwards and forwards, up and down – something he would be doing forty-eight years later on stage. By early 1959 Bob was performing as Elston Gunn and the Rock Boppers with a repertoire that blended doo-wop and rock'n'roll. In the summer of 1959 he also managed to talk himself into Bobby Vee's backing band the Shadows and pounded the piano for a couple of gigs.

Bobby Zimmerman's music-making was not unusual. Many young people around the world formed bands at school in the wake of rock'n'roll. Yet there was a characteristic of Bob's early approach to performing that has been commented upon by those who witnessed it: he did not seem unduly concerned about rehearsal. As Sounes comments,

> In later life, Bob became notorious in the music business for performing improvisational shows after sketchy rehearsals or no rehearsals at all. This unusual, almost jazz like approach helped him remain a fresh and dynamic performer, but it sometimes drove his band members to distraction. He was just as relaxed about rehearsals back in high school. Bucklen [friend and band member] recalls that Elston Gunn and his Rock Boppers did not rehearse together even once for their show. Bob was relaxed enough to go out on stage and see what happened. (2001: 62)

While Bob Dylan has spent a lot of time alone, learning to play music (listening to recordings, playing instruments) and writing songs, the skills he has acquired and the songs he has learned and written exist to be brought to an audience, not to be perfected in a rehearsal room or studio. His playing always had to be a performance for someone – his father, mother and grandmother; his girlfriend and her parents; his high school friends; and eventually the unknown public in concert halls and at festivals. As he remembered, "I needed to play for people all the time. You can say I practiced in public and my whole life was becoming what I practiced" (Dylan 2004: 16).

After leaving high school Bob enrolled at the University of Minnesota in September 1959. Although nominally studying music as his major subject, he attended very few classes and eventually dropped out, but it was in Minneapolis–St. Paul that he became inspired by folk music. After hearing Odetta's highly rhythmic acoustic gospel-influenced folk, he swapped his electric guitar for a good-quality acoustic guitar. This allowed him to perform in the clubs and coffee-bars of the bohemian Dinkytown area. As an acoustic guitar player with a repertoire of folk music, he extended his technique of practising in public. Numerous people who were around at the time, cited in various articles and memoirs, are emphatic in stressing how he performed seemingly without regard for those who didn't like his style of singing and stage manner. Dylan recalled, "I'd either drive people away or they'd come in closer to see what it was all about. There was no in-between" (2004: 18). One of his biographers concurs about this period: "Very few people felt lukewarm about Dylan; they either loved or hated him" (Shelton 1986: 116). This encapsulates Dylan's relationship with audiences throughout his life as a performer. Anecdotes recounted by fans I have met over the years tell a story of curious audience members attending only one show and being driven away, whilst others have been captivated and keep coming back.

The folk aesthetic that he now embraced as Bob Dylan was quite different from the rock'n'roll that he had been playing. Acoustic sound was valued; folk ideology rejected the mass culture of television, Hollywood movies and electric pop music. The folk crowd romanticized the outsider, the oppressed and the bohemian in opposition to the complacent conformity of middle-class affluence. To be taken seriously, to be an authentic folk singer, required a particular type of self-presentation. Out of necessity – to become an insider, to gain credibility – Bob began concealing details about his background while making up a range of often highly colourful biographical tales, including stories about running away from home, itinerant travelling, working in circuses and even being an orphan. He was not lying from vanity or conceit, nor was it a coherent and calculated attempt to create the Bob Dylan persona. Many of his stories were far too implausible and inconsistent. His strategy (if it can be called that), at least initially, was both pragmatic and defensive. He was seeking to obscure the fact that this scruffy kid, singing blues and old ballads with a nasal voice and badly tuned guitar, was actually a clean-cut young man from a middle-class Jewish household. Those who got to know him were very soon aware of these fictions, and once he began releasing albums it didn't take long for a journalist to "expose" details of his family background in a sarcastic article in *Newsweek* in November 1963.

If he'd called himself Elston Gunn to sound rock'n'roll and performed in suitable rock'n'roll attire, then he was equally aware that the bohemian folk singer Bob Dylan would need more than just the name. Yet he was also seeking something that answered a deeper need. He was at the age when many people who have recently left their family home are asking themselves just who they are, now that they are out in the world on their own. He initially found inspiration in Woody Guthrie's memoir *Bound for Glory*. He was captivated with the life, identity and music of Guthrie, just as he had been enamoured of Little Richard. He began to imitate Guthrie's guitar-playing and vocal style, he dressed like him, he absorbed the Oklahoma inflection of Guthrie's speaking voice. As he sang them, Dylan began to identify with the subjects and characters of Guthrie's songs; he connected with the way Guthrie gave a voice to the underdog, the downtrodden and the dispossessed.

Dylan's infatuation with Guthrie came at a moment when he was seeking direction and questioning his own identity. Shelton remarks that "the change of summer 1960 grew out of a genuine need for a new identity" and he quotes two friends: Gretel Hoffman remembering, "He was very open about it. He explained that he was building a character"; and Tony Glover adding, "He said it was an act, but only for about two days. He said: 'After that, it was me'" (Shelton 1986: 75).

Here again it is possible to overstate the novelty and the calculated wisdom of the adoption of a Bob Dylan persona. Some writers have described the bohemian folk singer as a role, a claim most bluntly asserted by

Larry Smith, who portrays it as a pose used during what he rather cynically calls Dylan's "folk-posturing period" (2005: 17). More plausible is Shelton's view that it was an extension of his character. Dylan was comfortable being "studiously unkempt" (1986: 108). He happily adopted a hip, beat-inflected argot and folk style. But acting out the part of bohemian folk singer was not going to lead very far unless he could make an impact as a musician.

It was in Minneapolis that Dylan really developed his acoustic guitar-playing. He began to find a distinct singing voice, he worked hard on his harmonica-playing and began tentatively doodling around with his own versions of folk songs. He was in Minneapolis–St. Paul for just over a year. In December 1960 he evidently decided that it was time to move on. He arrived in New York City about a week later. From New York he would be able to visit Woody Guthrie (who was ill in a New Jersey hospital suffering from Huntington's chorea), and he would also have more opportunities for contact with record companies.

Becoming a recording artist

Dylan's life in Greenwich Village has been recounted on many occasions (Shelton 1986; Hajdu 2002; Van Ronk 2006). He began playing in the small folk clubs and coffee-houses and quickly established a presence in the far from unified folk scene. As always, he would drive some people away. He voraciously absorbed much of the music and culture of New York. He was reading widely, he was listening to a lot of folk music on record and in the clubs, he was watching and talking to blues singers, he was thinking about the phrasing and dynamics used by jazz musicians, particularly when they were performing with rhythmically delivered beat poetry, he was attending theatres and cinemas, and generally reflecting on the structure of popular songs and dynamics of performance.

Just ten months after arriving in New York City, in October 1961, Dylan signed a contract with Columbia Records. His first album, *Bob Dylan*, was recorded over two afternoons in November and released in March 1962. It did not sell very well, and it is said that many staff at Columbia Records were sceptical of his potential. But it got him greater recognition, it boosted his confidence and it gave him momentum and the motivation to develop his own songwriting. His second album, *The Freewheelin' Bob Dylan*, is generally recognized as a major recording in popular music history. In 2006, forty-five years later, Bob Dylan released *Modern Times*, his thirty-second studio-recorded album for Columbia. Apart from a brief moment during the early 1970s when he was negotiating for better terms and released *Planet Waves* and *Before The Flood* on Asylum (subsequently assigned to Columbia), Dylan has always been a Columbia recording artist.

The music business is often spoken of pejoratively as a corporate machine, an industry that sucks in talent, chews it up and spits it out. Anyone who has been given a hard time by record companies will know that this is an apt metaphor. However, professional creative musicians who have been around as long as Bob Dylan tend to have experienced the music business less as an abstract processing machine and more as a series of relationships with particular people. Their artistic career and development of musicianship have often been assisted by specific people, and disputes that have led to the courtroom have concerned the incompetence or devious practice of individuals (and not the automated workings of a machine). Considering how much has been written about Dylan, there has been little detail about his business dealings. In scratching the surface of a large and under-researched subject, all I want to do here is to highlight three key industry people (from many) who played an important part in Dylan's early commercial career as a contracted musician.

I have already mentioned Robert Shelton at various points in this chapter, as I have been frequently drawing on his biography (Shelton 1986). Shelton was the folk music critic for the *New York Times* when Dylan was trying to establish himself in Greenwich Village. Having become an acquaintance of Dylan's, he wrote a review of a performance at Gerde's Folk City that appeared in the newspaper on 29 September 1961 under the headline "Bob Dylan: A Distinctive Folksong Stylist". The review was important recognition, signalling Dylan's talent within the folk world and to a wider circle of readers. It was also noticed by personnel in the record companies. In a succinct article Shelton captured key features of Dylan's style at this moment. He wrote of him as

> a cross between a choir boy and a beatnik ... Mr. Dylan's voice is anything but pretty. He is consciously trying to recapture the rude beauty of a Southern field hand musing in melody on his back porch. All the "husk and bark" are left on his notes, and a searing intensity pervades his songs.

Shelton described Dylan as "bursting at the seams with talent", noted that he was vague about his background and concluded that "it matters less where he has been than where he is going, and that would seem to be straight up" (1986: 111). A few months later, under the pseudonym Stacey Williams, Shelton would be writing the liner notes to Dylan's debut album.

Dylan was very excited about the review, and attendances at his performances increased sharply. For Shelton it was the beginning of a relatively close relationship with Dylan. He frequently spoke at length with the musician and was given access to his parents. Although they seemed to drift apart during the 1970s, Shelton's biography benefits from the access he had to Dylan in the ten-year period after the review was published, and is particularly strong on his family background. It was shortly after Shelton's review appeared that Dylan signed with Columbia Records, and it is generally agreed that the review played a part in convincing the company's executive John Hammond that he was doing the right thing in signing Dylan. There are conflicting stories about whether Hammond had seen Dylan live, and questions about his familiarity with Bob's repertoire, and the extent to which he acted in response to Shelton's eulogy. Even if there was no direct causal link, Shelton was vocal in folk circles in drawing attention to Dylan's talents. Liam Clancy thought that Shelton "more than anyone, was responsible for Bob Dylan. He pushed and pushed and pushed" (Heylin 2001: 75). Shelton himself believed Hammond's decision was driven by instinct and an awareness of Dylan's growing reputation; it was an intuitive judgement.

John Hammond was born in 1910 into a wealthy family and studied the violin at Yale before dropping out and taking up music journalism. With the economic support of his family, he became involved in promoting and recording jazz and blues musicians and joined Columbia Records in 1958. He has been characterized as an old-style "music man", who set out to "discover" talent, his aspirations artistic rather than primarily financial. His motives were also undoubtedly liberal; he wrote for a left-leaning journal *New Masses* and he supported a large number of black artists in various ways. He recognized the significance of the music of Bessie Smith and Billie Holiday, along with Count Basie, Lionel Hampton, Benny Carter, Lester Young and Aretha Franklin. Hammond provided a link between the pre-war world of jazz and blues and the post-war folk revival and development of rhythm and blues and rock music. He was associated with Pete Seeger, then Leonard Cohen, and in later years with Bruce Springsteen. Hammond was respected for his judgement throughout the music industry, and Dylan was well aware of the significance of being signed by such a figure.

A third character entered the story just after Dylan signed with Columbia. This was Albert Grossman, who would become Dylan's manager from August 1962 until 1971. Subsequently, during the early 1980s, the pair were involved in lawsuits about royalties and payments. Grossman had been promoting folk singers and had jointly set up the Newport Folk Festival, astutely recognizing that the 1950s folk movement would have broader public appeal. He was managing Odetta, which impressed Dylan, and clearly believed that Dylan could become a major music star beyond the folk world. Grossman initially attempted to get Dylan out of his recording contract, realizing that the musician had been less than twenty-one years old when he committed himself to Columbia. Grossman insisted that Dylan allow him to negotiate another contract on his behalf. As Dylan recalls:

> Hammond had believed in me and had backed up his belief, had given me my first start on the world's stage, and no one, not even Grossman, had anything to do with that. There was no way I'd go against him for Grossman, not in a million years. I knew that the contract would have to be straightened out, though, so I went to see him. The mere mention of Grossman's name just about gave him apoplexy. (2004: 289–90)

Grossman was equally furious that Dylan's ethics and loyalty to Hammond had led him to re-sign to Columbia without negotiating a better deal. Columbia contested Grossman's claim by arguing that Dylan had confirmed the contract by recording for the company after the age of twenty-one (Hammond 1977). Eventually a compromise was worked out and the three parties – Dylan, Grossman and Columbia – worked together. Grossman played an important role in the transition that saw Bob Dylan move from a folk singer to an international rock star. Whilst the manager would often keep a low profile and insisted to Shelton that Dylan would have made it, with or without him, there can be little doubt that he contributed to Dylan's success.

Grossman recognized the importance of Dylan's, songs and encouraged him to write more. As a businessman on a percentage of Dylan's earnings, he realized their publishing potential. Not only could more money be made from cover versions by better-known artists, such as Grossman's other act Peter, Paul and Mary, who had a hit with 'Blowin' In The Wind', but these renditions would also publicize Dylan as a songwriter.

At a time when few popular performers wrote their own material, Grossman also recognized the value of the critical acclaim Dylan was gaining for his songwriting. Grossman understood that Dylan was a new type of popular musician and he was concerned with maintaining his image of artistic integrity as well as exploiting his commercial potential (realizing that the two were not mutually exclusive). Grossman did not allow Dylan to be promoted as a typical popular musician, in cheap gossip magazines and lightweight television shows. Bob Dylan was, in general, presented as an artist who should be taken seriously.

When Grossman is mentioned in biographies of Dylan he often appears as a rather devious and shadowy figure, with little appreciation of the part he played in Dylan's success as a musician. Shelton implies that Grossman influenced Dylan's aesthetic direction in a subtle and understated manner, although he is rather vague about how he did this. The film-maker D. A. Pennebaker thought that one of Grossman's major contributions was to keep Dylan focused because he had a tendency to "go off at spurious tangents" (Heylin 2000: 97). Dylan would stay pretty focused until 1966. After that, he did indeed go off on spurious tangents. Whether or not it had anything to do with Grossman's declining influence, he would be all the more interesting for it.

2 Chronologies

The first album, simply titled *Bob Dylan*, provides the merest hint of the material that Dylan was performing at the time in folk clubs and coffee-houses. More can be heard on *The Bootleg Series Volumes 1–3 (Rare & Unreleased) 1961–1991* and on unreleased recordings circulating among collectors. Although Dylan's vocal style, guitar-playing and choice of songs on *Bob Dylan* clearly signalled his debt to the blues, the two self-written songs are an unequivocal acknowledgement of the influence of Woody Guthrie. 'Talkin' New York' is a light, talking blues, a song Dylan rarely performed after this time. In contrast, 'Song To Woody' signals the emergence of a serious songwriter, commenting on the hardship of Guthrie's life and the people he sought to represent. Dylan acknowledges this specific debt whilst paying homage to other folk-blues singers (naming Leadbelly and Cisco Houston). Based on a lilting traditional tune that Guthrie had used in '1913 Massacre', the song would stay in Dylan's live repertoire and be performed almost unchanged over the next forty years.

Dylan began recording for his second album within a month of the first being released. He completed a number of sessions, stretched out across the year and the resulting album *The Freewheelin' Bob Dylan* was issued in May 1963. During this period Dylan had been performing and writing constantly, the songs often taking shape as they were refined in front of an audience. *Freewheelin'* also represents only part of Dylan's repertoire at the time, and a number of good songs didn't make it onto the album, including 'Talkin' John Birch Society Paranoid Blues', a slapstick satire on anti-Communism; 'Let Me Die In My Footsteps', an anti-nuclear meditation on the proliferation of bomb shelters; 'The Death Of Emmett Till', a commentary on the racial murder of a black youth; and 'Walls Of The Red Wing', a first-person tale of life in a remand home.

Freewheelin' is one of Bob Dylan's most important albums. His first album had given little indication of what was to come and many of his peers in the folk scene were surprised by the quality and range of Dylan's writing. The album began with the questioning, spiritual 'Blowin' In The Wind', took the listener through heartfelt remembrance of lost love in 'Girl From The North Country', presented sloganeering protest in 'Masters Of War', and introduced 'A Hard Rain's A-Gonna Fall', a moody epic of dystopian anxiety woven together with extraordinary combinations of rhyme, rhythm and symbolism. Dylan sang of the ambivalent mix of tenderness and bitterness that can accompany the parting of lovers in 'Don't Think Twice, It's All Right', he agitated for Civil Rights in the consciousness-raising commentary of 'Oxford Town', and he satirized musical form and political paranoia in 'Talkin' World War III Blues'. He evoked the mysterious dream logic of memories in 'Bob Dylan's Dream' (the first of many dream songs), he hollered the blues in 'Down The Highway', and included three joyous jokey songs, 'Bob Dylan's Blues', 'Honey, Just Allow Me One More Chance' (a traditional number), and 'I Shall Be Free'. Ever since, Dylan's songwriting has always ranged widely from the frivolous to the profound, from outward-looking observation to inward-looking absorption.

There is a richness and range to Dylan's guitar-playing on this album. He uses delicate finger-picking, varied shades of rhythmic strumming, different tunings (mainly variants on open D) and a range of "inverted" chord shapes that are more typical of folk and Delta blues than pop. Right from the earliest days of his life as a professional musician Dylan was not simply strumming basic triadic chord shapes, he was thinking about tuning and fingering and how this gives a very particular timbre and texture to his songs. He would continue to use different guitar tunings throughout the 1960s and into the early 1970s.

Freewheelin' includes a traditional ballad 'Corrina, Corrina', one of a number of performances at the time that were recorded with a band of guitar, bass, piano and drums. In the previous December, a bluesy, rockabilly shuffle 'Mixed-Up Confusion' had been issued as a single, although this was subsequently withdrawn. Outtakes from the *Freewheelin'* sessions also include band versions of 'Rocks And Gravel' and an Elvis-like version of Arthur Crudup's 'That's Alright Mama'. While Dylan was performing in public as a folk musician with acoustic guitar and harmonica, his love of electric blues and rock'n'roll is evident from the single and the tracks that were not included on the album. The decision to release 'Mixed-Up Confusion' as a single indicates that neither Dylan nor Columbia Records assumed that he was restricted to acoustic music. Dylan was never a pure folk singer, and the musical and lyrical depth to this second album has been continually emphasized as he has rearranged the songs when performing with other musicians in different circumstances.

The first song on the album, 'Blowin' In The Wind', is one of his best known and has been performed by countless artists since Peter, Paul and Mary had a hit with it in the summer of 1963. Asked about the song in the late 1970s, Dylan said, "I think I'll always be able to do that. There are certain songs that I will always be able to do. They will always have just as much meaning, if not more, as time goes by" (Rosenbaum 1978: 82). The song has indeed stayed with him, still being performed in 2007. In concert with Joan Baez during 1975 it had been pushed up to G, the higher-pitched vocals and the more rhythmic and faster pace of the delivery conveying greater optimism about finding the answers that are blowing in the wind. By 2000 Dylan was performing the song at a much slower pace, pitched a tone lower in C and sung as an almost world-weary, melancholic lament for that ever-elusive answer that might still be out in the breeze somewhere.

'A Hard Rain's A-Gonna Fall' has undergone similar changes of emphasis. The *Freewheelin'* version, delivered with the understated pendulum swing of a traditional ballad, conveys anxiety about the future through images of innocence betrayed, hopes thwarted, opportunities unrealized, warnings unheeded; the repeated hook of "hard, hard, hard, hard, hard" emphasizes the need for perseverance in the face of hardship and impending catastrophe. In 1975, on the Rolling Thunder Revue tour, the song was also raised in pitch (from E to A) and performed as a 4/4 galloping rock boogie. Dylan's declamatory, assertive singing suggests a greater sense of defiance, strength and endurance – perhaps claiming back the song after Brian Ferry had warbled his way through a superficial rendition, complete with glib sound effects, two years earlier. One of Dylan's most expressive versions, and one of the most politically poignant performances, was at the Todaiji Temple, in Nara, Japan, with the Tokyo New Philharmonic Orchestra in May 1994. There is a redemptive, hymnlike quality to this performance, as the restrained intonation of Dylan's words blends with shimmering orchestral textures and seems to summon the ghosts of those who suffered the very real hard rain in Hiroshima and Nagasaki.

The continuing relevance of those who profit as 'Masters Of War' has been apparent over the years since it was first recorded. Dylan has performed this song both solo on acoustic guitar and with a variety of bands, and in two quite distinct guises. He has continually returned to the stark 6/8 ballad style of *Freewheelin'* whilst also performing a more straightforward 4/4 rock shuffle version. Lyrically unsubtle but politically ambiguous, Dylan has always seemed concerned with the general futility of war (rather than specific ideological positions and conflicts), along with the moral emptiness of those who benefit from the sufferings of soldiers and their victims. The song evokes generalities and universals that can be applied to different circumstances, and listeners have continually interpreted the song according to local political beliefs. When the song featured live in the USA not long after the attack on Manhattan in September 2001, some members of the audience apparently shouted "Death to Bin Laden!" (Marqusee 2003: 1). By the time Dylan was performing it during 2005 and 2006 in the UK, delivered with an almost funereal rhythm, it was cheered as a comment on the involvement of British and US armed forces in Iraq.

© RB/Redferns

The protest singer 1963

Another song that has endured in concerts is 'The Times They Are A-Changing', released in January 1964 on the album that followed *Freewheelin'*. The first and title song of the album *The Times They Are A-Changin'*, it was a calculated attempt to write an anthem, as Dylan later recalled: "I wanted to write a big song, some kind of theme song ... the civil rights movement and the folk music movement were pretty close and allied together for a while at that time" (Crowe 1985: 43). The song quickly became an opening statement of intent at Dylan's concerts during this period. With Joan Baez, Dylan had sung 'Blowin' In The Wind' and 'Only A Pawn In Their Game' at the Freedom March in Washington on 28 August 1963, the event at which Dr Martin Luther King made his famous "I have a dream" speech. Dylan was making an important public stand as part of a movement of white liberal musicians, artists and writers adding their voices to the struggle for civil rights. Many of the songs on the album are attempts to raise awareness and to publicize the campaign for civil rights, as were many of Dylan's performances during this period.

Although Dylan has continued to perform the title song, 'The Times They Are A-Changin' ', some critics have heard it as an empty gesture towards a bygone era, its appearance in concerts dismissed as a "meaningless Greatest Hit" (Gray 2006: 662). Only fourteen years after its first release, in 1978, Michael Gray was hearing the version that appeared on *Bob Dylan At Budokan* as "a sad, slow admission of his generation's failure ... there is even the inspired touch of a Duane Eddy guitar-sound to emphasize the song's anachrony" (*ibid.*). The song's political irrelevance seemed confirmed for some disappointed fans in 1994 when Dylan allowed the accountancy firm Coopers & Lybrand to use it in an advertising campaign, with the chorus appropriated as a corporate catchphrase to show how the firm was helping business respond to changes in manufacturing, investment and organization. Yet the light, relaxed, bluegrass-tinged version that appeared in Dylan's concerts during 1999 and 2000 did not resonate with the forlorn hopes of the 1960s, nor with the brusque swagger of 1990s big business. Its mellow folk tones and leisurely pace, along with Dylan's softly intoned, gnarled voice of observation, rather than participation, made it sound like a ballad that had been around for a couple of hundred years or more, speaking to and of all manner of historical changes.

Over the years, Dylan has reinterpreted other songs from *The Times They Are A-Changin'*, emphasizing the bleak intensity of 'Ballad Of Hollis Brown' and the heart-rending yearning of 'Boots Of Spanish Leather'. Even 'The Lonesome Death Of Hattie Carroll' has transcended its origins in early 1960s protest. The ballad dramatizes a newspaper report about a rich, white real estate magnate who attacked a black kitchen maid with such a ferocity that she died of her injuries. Yet he only received a sentence of manslaughter and served just three months in prison. Initially delivered as a consciousness-raising call for action, forty years later it had become a sombre lament reminding audiences of the brutality and injustices that were such a prominent feature of the very recent past.

Sometimes overlooked amongst the "protest" of *The Times They Are A Changin'* is one of Dylan's most reflective, soft and introspective performances on 'One Too Many Mornings', a song sketching the sounds and images of the city as dusk falls and the singer feels an unrequited nostalgic longing for a love that has gone. This is another song that he would still be playing live over forty years later.

Dylan's campaigning for civil rights made him popular with the New Left student movement and he was treated as both public spokesman and political visionary (see Garman 2000). Regardless of his commitment to human rights and racial equality, Dylan had no desire to be part of a left political agenda and no wish to be treated as a public spokesman, even less a prophet. *Another Side Of Bob Dylan*, released just six months later, included one of his most important songs, 'My Back Pages' – an unequivocal renunciation of the protest song, in which he takes the satire that he has directed at others and turns it on himself, denouncing his earlier earnestness, castigating a moral agenda which sees the world in black and white, exposing his confusion and self-doubt, ridiculing the preaching tone that was turning him into the sort of person he despised. All this is sealed with an instantly memorable chorus that inverts an everyday cliché about being older and wiser as "I was so much older then, I'm younger than that now".

With a casual and relaxed feel, the album features the first publicly available recording of Dylan's bluesy piano-playing on 'Black Crow Blues' and once more ranges from the light and jokey ('I Shall Be Free No. 10', 'Motorpsycho Nitemare') to the intensely personal ('Ballad In Plain D'). The songs continually address questions about personal freedom, but there is no social commentary or protest. There is a discernible air of renunciation, of mistrust, of suspicion, of leave-me-alone, don't-follow-me. The closing track, 'It Ain't Me, Babe', is ostensibly about a failing romantic relationship but has, with some justification, been heard as a song addressed to an audience seeking a martyr who will "protect you and defend you whether you are right or wrong ... someone who will die for you and more". The declamatory chorus "No, no, no, it ain't me, babe" is directed at the clinging left audience in search of a leader as much as it seeks release from the clutches of a female protagonist in the lyrical narrative.

Reels of rhyme and waves of sound

Bringing It All Back Home was released in March 1965, followed by *Highway 61 Revisited* just five months later. Sandwiched between them was Dylan's appearance with a band at the Newport Folk Festival, a much-discussed performance of just three songs that has been written into popular music history as the moment when he symbolically "went electric" and sonically disavowed folk protest in a far more dramatic manner than in the words of 'My Back Pages'. From the summer of 1965 to the end of May 1966 many (but not all) of Dylan's performances would be greeted with a mixed reaction, in which a vocal minority were booing, slow handclapping and heckling. From the various accounts of this period, it is clear that Dylan attracted equal amounts of reverence and hostility. He continued to divide audiences; listeners either wanted to stay or he drove them away.

Dylan had always loved rock'n'roll and electric blues and when he first heard the Beatles in 1964 he had something of an epiphany:

> "We were driving through Colorado, we had the radio on, and eight of the Top 10 songs were Beatles songs ... 'I Wanna Hold Your Hand,' all those early ones. They were doing things nobody was doing. Their chords were outrageous, just outrageous, and their harmonies made it all valid. You could only do that with other musicians ... I knew they were pointing the direction of where music had to go." (Heylin 2000: 148).

The Beatles inspired Dylan to think about how his songs would sound with a band of musicians, as did the Byrds' versions of his songs, particularly

'Mr. Tambourine Man' (released prior to Dylan's recording of the song) and the Animals' 'House Of The Rising Sun' (producer Tom Wilson tried, unsuccessfully, to overdub electric instruments onto Dylan's acoustic version of this song). But Dylan didn't suddenly embrace the type of chords and sequences that the Beatles were using, nor did he go for Beatles-type harmonies. The Beatles' assimilation of gospel, soul and rhythm and blues into their sound was far sweeter than Dylan's, and was mixed with mainstream 1950s pop and British vaudeville. Dylan's incorporation of the same influences was harder and tougher, blended with the blues and ballad traditions.

The first seven tracks on *Bringing It All Back Home* were recorded with a band of electric guitars, bass and drums, with Bruce Langhorne's lightly picked electric guitar on the eighth track ('Mr. Tambourine Man') providing a transition to the three closing tracks performed on acoustic guitar. Once again, the album displays the range of Dylan's songwriting, from the slapstick country shuffle of 'Bob Dylan's 115th Dream', through tender, delicately performed love songs ('Love Minus Zero/ No Limit'), to more general complaints about institutions and conformity ('Subterranean Homesick Blues' and 'Maggie's Farm'). The focused targets of his protest songs (racial

© Jan Persson/Redferns

Performing in Stockholm 1966

oppression, the plight of the poor) are superseded by a more nebulous in-group sense of "us" (the hip bohemians) against "them" (straight society). The album includes four outstanding songs: 'She Belongs To Me', an ironic title for a blues about a self-possessed woman who belongs to no one, a lover refusing the possessiveness of romantic love; the hallucinatory 'Mr. Tambourine Man', one of Dylan's most memorable and unusual melodies; the epic 'It's Alright, Ma (I'm Only Bleeding)', a song that condenses social critique and existential anxiety into a stream of quotable, proverb-like lines; and 'It's All Over Now, Baby Blue', another song that has been heard as addressed to the political left and folk crowd, as much as the lyrics suggest a parting from a friend or lover.

On *Bringing It All Back Home* Dylan increased his experiments with words, adopting an approach influenced by notions of spontaneous free association, surrealism, the art of the absurd, and images of the grotesque. Nigel Williamson is typical of many critics when he argues that 'Love Minus Zero/ No Limit' brought "fresh depths to the moon-in-June banalities that characterized pop romance at the time" (2004: 204). It is debatable whether pop romance of the time could be characterized in such limited, stereo-typical terms, particularly in light of the gospel-inflected soul being created by the Stax, Atlantic and Motown record labels and the songs coming out of Britain from the Who, Kinks, Rolling Stones and Beatles. Even if the vocabulary of romantic pop was in such a clichéd state, Dylan's alternative included plenty of clunky phrases like "In ceremonies of the horsemen, even the pawn must hold a grudge". It doesn't quite tumble from the tongue like moon and June, but it is also a song, so it is gone in a moment.

The stream-of-consciousness, unedited and intuitive quality of Dylan's lyrical experiments are readily apparent on *Highway 61 Revisited*, where the juxtaposition of images can be provocative and profound, arch and preten-tious, self-effacingly witty and caustically comic, and banal all within a few seconds. The imagery in the songs, impelled by his obsessive rhyming, conveys a sense of life around Dylan as a careening carnival populated by shifty and shifting characters, a distorted world where nothing is quite as it seems. The recurrent slightly off-kilter, stumbling, echoey, honky-tonk piano adds to the disorientation, as the familiar becomes strange and the strange disturbingly familiar.

The sound of *Highway 61 Revisited* was as important as the words. The rich musical texture, drawn from 1950s pop, blues, and rhythm and blues, seems indebted, whether consciously or not, to the dense "wall of sound" created by producer Phil Spector on a range of early 1960s pop songs. By using larger than normal ensembles, combining electric and acoustic instruments, and feeding reverberation back into the recording as it was taking place, Spector immersed and buried individual instruments in an overall texture rather than allowing specific instruments to stand out with clarity.

After he had fallen out with Tom Wilson, who produced his previous three albums, Dylan actually suggested Spector as a possible producer. Mark Polizzotti assumes that Dylan was being "sarcastic" (2006: 78) and Clinton Heylin comments, "What Phil Spector would have made of *Highway 61* I fear to speculate" (2000: 217). This scepticism seems misplaced. Not long after the album was released, Dylan and Spector became acquainted and spent some time hanging out and discussing music together. They clearly respected each other's work (Shelton 1986). Spector went on to produce the best solo work of John Lennon ('Instant Karma', 'Power To The People', *Imagine*, *Some Time In New York City*) and George Harrison (*All Things Must Pass*). Latterly, the production on Bruce Springsteen's *Born In The USA* is hugely indebted to both Spector's wall of sound and Dylan's mid-1960s instrumental textures. There's more than a hint of Spector's recording aesthetic on *Highway 61 Revisited*.

Although Bob Johnson, the Columbia staff producer, oversaw the recording of *Highway 61*, from all accounts Dylan was involved in very actively directing the recording and mixing of the album. The production, recorded more or less live, creates a similar overall texture to that of Spector. It is perhaps less relentless than Spector's wall, more a sea of sound with continual waves, in which the lyrics too float in and out as passing images rather than stanzas of verse. The inspired musical gestures of individual musicians frequently rise to the surface – Mike Bloomfield's searing, metallic, electric guitar licks; Paul Griffin's devotional embellishments on piano; Al Kooper's swirling organ; Dylan's characteristic high-pitched, insistent harmonica. But it is the overall sonic texture that so often strikes listeners when they first encounter the album – the strummed acoustic guitar with abrasive, electric blues guitar; the acoustic piano playing honky-tonk and blues patterns with the electric organ playing gospel-inspired swirls, stabs and swells; the shuffling train rhythms from the drums; the rooted yet undulating bass.

The album contains some of Dylan's most celebrated and much performed songs, opening with 'Like A Rolling Stone' – a scornful portrayal of a spoilt rich woman who can't comprehend her own decline, yet also a liberating, joyful anthem of independence, the chorus "How does it feel?" exclaimed over a repeated three-chord sequence (C,F,G,F) that had been popularized in Ritchie Valens' 1958 version of the traditional Mexican folk dance 'La Bamba'. During subsequent performances of 'Like A Rolling Stone' it has become clear just how skilled Dylan is in using the same song to convey different emotions: the message created less by the semantics of the lyrics than by their intonation and the musical arrangement. The song – directed at a "you" – can sound like a withering put-down, a sympathetic assertion of solidarity, a melancholic lament of regret, or a communal exaltation of joy. On *Bob Dylan At Budokan* Wilfrid Mellers heard the song "transformed from a gleeful song of rejection into a powerful, almost hymnic paean which has only a vicarious connection with the words" (1984: 219).

The other enduring put-down song from the album is 'Ballad Of A Thin Man', which blends Dylan's sarcastic commentary directed at the bewildered Mr Jones, who "knows something is happening" but doesn't know what it is, with imagery drawn from Dylan's memories of seeing geeks and freaks at carnivals during the 1950s (inspiration for the song which Dylan recounted on stage at the Charlotte Coliseum, North Carolina, on 19 December 1978). Propelled by Dylan's stalking, accusatory piano, pervaded by spooky Wurlitzer-like organ flourishes straight out of suspense or horror movies, and punctuated by touches of trebley, twanging guitar reminiscent of Westerns and mysteries, the band are creating a soundtrack to a movie, as much as an arrangement of a song (as they do during the noirish tale of estrangement recounted in 'Just Like Tom Thumb's Blues' and in the litany of bizarre incidents that feature in 'Highway 61 Revisited').

The sea of sound evaporates for the album's final track, the long, rambling 'Desolation Row', its tableau of gloomy and grotesque characters counterbalanced by Charlie McCoy's lightly picked, ornamental, chiming, acoustic guitar lines. Over the years the lyrics to this song have been subject to endless analysis in books, journals, magazines and fanzines. At the time, the response to the lyrics of this song, and to *Highway 61 Revisited* in general, was a clear sign of how Dylan was not only distancing himself from traditional folk music and the political left, but was also moving away from a working-class culture associated with blues, country and rock'n'roll.

Dylan was being appreciated by a new faction of middle-class young people, excitedly embracing rock music as a new poetic art. He was no longer singing to and for the bohemian folk activists, but was connecting with listeners who were self-consciously seeking intellectual justification for their engagement with popular music. Betsy Bowden, who grew up listening to Dylan during the 1960s and published a book-length study in 1982, alluded to this when she described herself as a typical audience member at the time, "young, white and overeducated" (2001: 146). Dylan's lyrics had particular appeal for this audience, as Mike Marqusee recalled in an account of his experience as a Dylan fan during this period: "The sense that Dylan's songs contained coded messages to be deciphered by the hip cognoscenti ... actually made these songs powerfully attractive. Anything too upfront, too transparent, too easily accessible, could not be trusted" (2003: 139–40).

Dylan's songs were also considered "revolutionary" – a term that features repetitively in discussions of *Highway 61 Revisited* (Williamson 2004: Gray 2000); "the vagabond-poet-rebel inhabits our consciousness," wrote Robert Shelton (1986: 226). The mood is captured in Stephen Scobie's recollection of the excitement he and his peers felt when they heard 'Like A Rolling Stone': "There's never been a moment in the history of rock and roll to equal the excitement of that first sharp crack of the snare drum. Insistently, arrogantly, authoritatively, it inaugurated a new world" (2003: 122). The emergence, features and transient characteristics of that new world are mulled over at length in Greil Marcus's (2005) entire book celebrating this song.

Whether or not his music was bringing about social change, Dylan quickly began moving away from the rambling word-play of *Highway 61 Revisited* and by January 1966 was recording *Blonde On Blonde*, an album characterized by a more intimate and less declamatory tone. The words are less random, dealing far more with love, loss and longing, concerned with the multiple dimensions of human relationships rather than a carnival of characters. There is a wider range of musical references, still stitched together with the blues, but with the subtle melancholic hues of country music. This is the more ethereal, swirling "wild mercury sound", blending metallic electric and wooden acoustic guitar, tremolo organ, and a reedier, breathy harmonica. The effect is less abrasive, more restrained than *Highway 61 Revisited*. The songs range from the knockabout jokey marching-band blues of 'Rainy Day Women # 12 & 35' through the almost Beatles-ish pop of 'Absolutely Sweet Marie' to some of Dylan's greatest, heartfelt songs of desire, regret and romance – 'Visions Of Johanna', 'Sad-Eyed Lady Of The Lowlands' (a song never performed live), 'One Of Us Must Know (Sooner Or Later)' (very occasionally performed live) – complemented by Paul Griffin's undulating piano, and 'Just Like A Woman', on which Dylan manages to sound both tender and misogynistic.

Not long after finishing the album Dylan went on tour with the Hawks (soon to be renamed the Band). Available recordings indicate a marked contrast between the album about to be released and these stage performances. *Blonde On Blonde*, with its subtle, country-tinged blues, themes of romance, apology and loss, and featuring many songs intoned with a vulnerable, intimate voice, is in sharp contrast to the confrontational, claustrophobic performances with the Band. These catch the moment when a blues band is transmuting into a rock group, swept along on the adrenalin that is driving Dylan forward, and are a dense, dramatic contrast to the sparse acoustic sets with which Dylan opened the shows. It was a bold, theatrical juxtaposition to place before a largely unsuspecting audience. Once again, Dylan drove some people away, while others stayed.

Revising and romancing

For a brief moment in 1966 Bob Dylan seemed the archetypal rock singer, defining the style as an intelligent genre addressed to adults, leaving behind the inarticulate rebellion of rock'n'roll and the naïve romance of pop. Dylan's songs seemed pivotal, central to an emergent urbane, educated counter-culture that appreciated rock as a new form that was breaking down the distinction between high art and popular culture and offered an opportunity for existential expression, political statement and artistic rebellion.

Yet Dylan very quickly distanced himself from rock culture and began rediscovering and embracing the more direct appeal of folk, country, acoustic blues and 1950s pop. A minor motorcycle accident gave him the excuse to cancel a scheduled concert tour, retreat into the countryside and spend time with his young family, enjoying the ordinary pleasures of children's games, parties, trips out and vacations. He made music without needing to parade as Bob Dylan in press conferences and on stage. With the Band, at their Big Pink house, on a basic tape machine, he recorded numerous new songs, many semi-improvised. These typically ranged from the witty and frivolous ('Clothes Line Saga', 'Please, Mrs. Henry') to the weighty and profound ('Tears Of Rage', 'This Wheel's On Fire'). Recordings began circulating amongst musicians and eventually a selection was officially released as *The Basement Tapes* in 1975. The original recordings were remixed by Robbie Robertson and additional drums, guitar and piano were overdubbed. Dylan occasionally included some of these songs in performances during the 1990s and into the new millennium, and gave a pulsating version of 'Crash On The Levee (Down In The Flood)' a prominent place as the opening number in many concerts during 1995–6, subsequently re-recording this song for the film *Masked and Anonymous* in 2003.

With time to pause and think, Dylan reflected on how he had been using words in his songs and in 1968 he is reported to have told Allen Ginsberg: "What I'm trying to do is not too many words. There's no line you can stick your finger through, there's no hole in any of the stanzas. There's no blank filler. Each line has something" (Miles 1990: 392). Ginsberg explained further:

> "He wasn't just making up a line to go with a rhyme anymore;
> each line had to advance the story, bring the song forward …
> There was to be no wasted language, no wasted breath. All
> the imagery was to be functional rather than ornamental."
> (Heylin 2000: 287)

The results were apparent on *John Wesley Harding*, released at the end of 1967. Using the sparse instrumentation of acoustic guitar, piano and harmonica, with supporting bass and drums, Dylan economically sketched "a series of studies in allegory, psalm, parable, symbol, metaphor, and moral tale" (Shelton 1986: 389). The songs featured anonymous types (hobo, immigrant, messenger, drifter, landlord) in contrast to the flowery baroque characters of *Highway 61 Revisited*. *John Wesley Harding* includes Dylan's lyrically economical, musically sparse, and vocally understated performance of 'All Along The Watchtower', a song Jimi Hendrix quickly appropriated, stripping away the protagonist's ambivalence and the atmosphere of foreboding and turning it into a declamatory rock anthem. Dylan's subsequent live performances have been indebted to Hendrix's version – the only occasion when another performer has influenced how Dylan has re-imagined and chosen to perform his songs.

The countryish tinge that was becoming less disguised on *Blonde On Blonde* and *John Wesley Harding* burst into the open on *Nashville Skyline*, released in 1969. The liner notes were written by Johnny Cash, who joined Dylan for the opening duet of 'Girl From The North Country', the singers also appearing together on a couple of television shows. Just as Dylan's electric rendition of 'I Don't Believe You' shocked those familiar with the acoustic version and signalled his movement away from folk, so the casual, country revision of this familiar song framed an album that for many of his intellectual fans was disappointingly bereft of lyrics that could be analysed for hidden meanings. The contentment and joy of the music, Dylan's pleasure in singing about love and romance, also caused great discomfort to the New Left. It was thought to be "anodyne" and "harmless", full of lyrical clichés, his voice "a syrupy croon", some of the songs "inconsequential country hokum". Dylan was even criticized for looking like a "gormless country bumpkin on the cover" (Williamson 2004: 212). These complaints were mainly voiced by rock critics who wanted a Dylan that could be accommodated to their model of the literate, revolutionary, bohemian and prophetic artist. It is a narrow-minded take on country music, an unthinking dismissal of an album that, once again, rapidly changes mood from the profound sense of loss in 'I Threw It All Away' and the lover's anxiety of 'Tell Me That It Isn't True', through the good-time, knockabout domestic joy of 'Country Pie', to Dylan's most tender romantic seduction ballads 'Lay, Lady, Lay' and 'Tonight I'll Be Staying Here With You'. The warm, full textures and home-spun sentiments were in contrast to the stark instrumentation and bleak landscapes evoked on *John Wesley Harding*.

Critics uncomfortable with *Nashville Skyline* positively hated *Self Portrait*, a collection of covers of songs conventionally deemed light or middle-of-the-road, along with casually played live takes and lightly sketched folksy songs that were attributed to Dylan as composer, although he made little attempt to conceal their folk origins nor transform them through any poetic wordplay. The album featured over fifty musicians and vocalists, including a string section and brass. It dismayed those who preferred *their* Dylan to be rocking and revolutionary. Particularly galling was the inclusion of a performance of 'Like A Rolling Stone' recorded at the Isle of Wight Festival in August 1969, delivered with a lazy, country feel far removed from the bitterness and paranoia that seethes through the studio version. Pushed way up into the key of G (rather than C), Dylan's voice croons, leaps and scats as he stumbles through the lyrics. The song verges on becoming a hoe-down, a version for a barn dance rather than an anthem for the counter-culture. To release such a dramatically different interpretation, complete with "mistakes" (depending on your viewpoint), was a quite deliberate and provocative act. Dylan could have easily re-recorded the vocal line, or simply not released it. Clinton Heylin can barely conceal his rage as he fumes and moralizes: "The Isle of Wight version of 'Like A Rolling Stone,' his most famous song, is definitely a joke, and in very bad taste at that. He not only forgets the words, but strips the song of any feeling" (2000: 315).

Actually, this track and *Self Portrait* as a whole was a very good joke. Dylan cheekily released an album that was clearly not autobiographical with the title *Self Portrait* and put one of his best-ever musical jokes in the first song: 'All The Tired Horses' fades in with female singers chanting "all the tired horses in the sun, how'm I gonna get any ridin' done" before introducing some meandering Mantovani-esque strings that eventually settle us down into the easy chair. The song does not even feature Dylan's voice, let alone his characteristic wordplay, folk guitar, bluesy piano or harmonica. Like all good jokes it is both trivial and profound. It has been heard as a spontaneous fragment of lullaby that Dylan might have concocted while sending his children to sleep, and also as a calculated deconstruction of the Bob Dylan persona – the artist making himself invisible and inaudible in one of his own songs.

The joke was on those who got all worked up and angry with Dylan having a bit of musical fun. It poked a big hole in the naïve idea that a songwriter can have the answers to the world's woes. The derision and rage that greeted this pop record at the time now look quaint. Yet many fans (once again) felt justified in their feelings of betrayal as Dylan emphatically told them that neither the song 'Like A Rolling Stone' nor his music in general was going to inaugurate any new world.

Dylan was tired with the burden of responsibility that was being heaped upon him, irritated by the epithets of "prophet" and "spokesman of a generation". *Self Portrait* was a quite deliberate attempt to puncture the myths, put people off and send out a signal that Bob Dylan was not going to be typecast as a one-dimensional beat poet or rock rebel figure. The inclusion of Gordon Lightfoot's 'Early Mornin' Rain' and Rodgers and Hart's 'Blue Moon' indicated that his musical interests are wide and eclectic, cover all shades of the popular song, and are uninhibited by naïve ideological concerns about certain genres of music being more conservative or progressive than others.

Much of the next album, *New Morning* (1970), had the same casual, down-home rural feel, a quality that slightly belies the spiritual intensity of some of its gospel-inflected songs, particularly 'Three Angels' and 'Father Of Night'. The album commences with the ever-popular romantic 'If Not For You' – a big hit around the world for Olivia Newton-John in 1971 – just about the only song from the album that has consistently appeared live over the years. To the amazement of many fans Dylan's bluesy semi-improvised scat 'If Dogs Run Free' briefly appeared in a series of concerts for the first time during 2000. The country–gospel influence was again apparent on 'Knockin' On Heaven's Door', a song Dylan wrote for the soundtrack to *Pat Garrett and Billy the Kid* (1973), the film directed by Sam Peckinpah and featuring Dylan in a supporting role to James Coburn and Kris Kristofferson.

Dylan's rural retreat concluded with *Planet Waves* (1974), a collection characterized by a creeping unease, with darker and starker textures. The writing and recording of the album were both apparently rushed, leaving many of the unfinished-sounding songs to be developed later in concert. In particular, Dylan feels his way through two tentative versions of 'Forever Young', one slow and understated, the other almost a country dance. He later settled on a hymnlike country–gospel arrangement for this song, in which he sings of his hopes for the future of a young child (listen to the version on *Bob Dylan At Budokan*). *Planet Waves* marked a "reunion" of members of the Band and the album was followed by a tour of the United States.

The lack of subtlety that sometimes characterized the Hawks on tour during 1966 was compensated for by the fact that they were innovating, feeling their way ahead, working out what the conventions would become. By 1974 the conventions of rock had become set like concrete, and the live album from this tour, *Before The Flood*, documents some of the most bombastic performances by Bob Dylan and the Band. Whether or not it was due to a lack of adequate stage monitors in the huge arenas, Dylan shouts his way through most songs. Dylan himself subsequently described the tour as "superficial" (Williams 2004: 157) and his discomfort presumably infected the performances. As he recalled:

> "I think I was just playing a role on that tour. I was playing Bob Dylan and The Band was playing The Band. It was all sort of mindless. The people that came out to see us came mostly to see what they missed the first time around. It was just more of a "legendary" kind of thing ... Rock-and-roll had become a highly extravagant enterprise. T-shirts, concert booklets, lighting shows, costume changes, glitter and glamour – it was a big show, a big circus except there weren't any elephants, nothing really exceptional just Sound and Lights, Sound and Lights, and more Sound and Lights. ... The highest compliments were things like 'Wow, lotta energy, man'. It had become absurd. The bigger and louder something was, the more energy it was supposed to have ... The greatest praise we got on that tour was 'incredible energy, man', it would make me want to puke." (Crowe 1985: 24)

Extra textures

During the 1970s Dylan endured a traumatic separation from his first wife Sara, followed by a court case over custody of their children and ultimately a divorce in 1977. These personal difficulties did not provoke Dylan to bare his soul in autobiographical lyrics (at least not in songs that he ever put out publicly). Instead, they inspired him to find sometimes literal, but more usually figurative, ways of representing the range of emotions, situations and consequences of such strained human relations.

Dylan renewed his interest in song structures when he took a series of art lessons with Norman Raeben, which prompted him to approach his song lyrics as paintings, introducing a sense of perspective that allowed for the viewpoints of multiple protagonists and for constant shifting between present and past. At the same time, he extended his interest in guitar tunings – inspired by the music of and conversations with Joni Mitchell. This fed into a more general broadening of his sonic palette, and throughout the 1970s he began to use more varied rhythms and instrumentation, moving away from the mid-1960s organ/acoustic guitar texture and the informal acoustic folk, country, gospel and blues mixtures of the late 1960s. Dylan also became more interested in stagecraft and dramatic representation and this led directly to the highly theatrical Rolling Thunder Revue tour of 1975–76, during which he filmed a series of semi-structured, partly improvised dramatic episodes that were edited into the rambling four-hour film *Renaldo and Clara*, released in 1977.

Personal angst, a preoccupation with narrative and theatre, and experiments with more varied musical textures fed into three outstanding and contrasting albums between 1975 and 1978 (*Blood On The Tracks, Desire* and *Street Legal*), characterized lyrically by musings on time passing and lost love, linked to an ever more desperate mood of searching and estrangement. Across these three albums Dylan introduces a multi-layered approach to instrumentation and rhythms, moving through levels and exploring varied densities, from the prominence given to acoustic guitars on *Blood On The Tracks*, through the blending of thick, mournful, wailing harmonica and violin on *Desire*, to the spectral emptiness of the congas, lone saxophone and exposed organ on 'Where Are You Tonight?' (the final track of *Street Legal*).

The twinkling, country-tinged, folk blues of *Blood On The Tracks* permeates a collection of songs that almost uniformly deal with melancholic, sometimes bitter, reflections on the end of relationships, lost love and friendships, the experience of ageing, thwarted dreams and hopes betrayed. Dylan's use of open tuning results in constantly ringing open strings, with a timbre created by non-conventional chord fingerings (played higher up the neck), along with passing added sixth, extended ninth and eleventh, and major seventh chords. Together these musical features contribute to a breezy, lilting, shimmering ambience, counterbalancing the sadness conveyed by many of the lyrics.

The tracks for the album were initially recorded in New York with musicians from the band Deliverance, along with Paul Griffin on organ. After listening to an early test pressing and following discussions with his brother David, Dylan decided to re-record some of the songs in Minneapolis. There were four clear reasons for this. First, the initial album had a uniform sound, partly because all songs had been recorded in the key of E, and also due to Dylan's subdued mood and rather sombre vocals. Second, on a number of songs, the pitch seemed unsuitable for Dylan's voice and didn't allow the vocal to fully convey the sentiments of the song. Third, Dylan had decided to rewrite some of the lyrics. Fourth, it was felt that the record would have more chance of being played on the radio if it had a less introverted tone and brighter timbre. Dylan decided to release five songs that were recorded at the New York sessions – 'Simple Twist Of Fate', 'You're Gonna Make Me Lonesome When You Go', 'Meet Me In The Morning', 'Shelter From The Storm' and 'Buckets Of Rain'. He re-cut the other songs at sessions in Minneapolis arranged by David with musicians brought together by guitarist Kevin Odegard (Gill and Odegard 2004).

A test pressing had been manufactured and it wasn't long before the first New York versions began to circulate on bootlegs. Columbia Records eventually released takes of these, with the exception of 'Lily, Rosemary And The Jack of Hearts'. The contrasting recordings of the same songs give a rare insight into an artist reassessing his work.

The version of 'Tangled Up In Blue' that opens *Blood On The Tracks* was recorded in Minneapolis in the key of A, with triplets on a suspended fourth continually creating a tension and adding momentum, propelling the song forward. The New York version had been played in E, with the vocals pitched much lower, and there is less urgency, the performance more introverted. Dylan also re-recorded 'You're A Big Girl Now' and 'Idiot Wind' in Minneapolis, again both pitched higher than the New York version. From E they were raised to G and the greater tension in Dylan's voice as he reaches for higher pitches gives the singing and the songs' sentiments a less intro-spective feel. 'Lily, Rosemary And The Jack Of Hearts', initially recorded as a subdued solo acoustic number, was actually shifted down a tone in pitch from E to D for the country shuffle band version in Minneapolis, as was 'If You See Her, Say Hello'. On the New York recording of the latter song Dylan is straining, whereas the Minneapolis version, played in D, allows him to convey the sentiments of the song with a more relaxed and intimate vocal. These subtle changes, along with sprightly performances from the musicians, gave the album that was eventually released a greater range of musical details and more intricate emotional nuances than on the original test pressing.

Half the songs from *Blood On The Tracks* – 'Tangled Up In Blue', 'Simple Twist Of Fate', 'If You See Her, Say Hello', 'Shelter From The Storm', 'You're A Big Girl Now' – have continued to feature live into the mid-2000s. 'Tangled Up In Blue' has always been greeted enthusiastically by audiences and is evidently popular with Dylan, judging by the number of times he's played it. Apart from altering the song's lyrics, Dylan has varied the arrangement of 'Tangled Up In Blue' over the years, introducing a rhythmically staccato, electric blues version and a melancholic acoustic blues rendition. Alex Ross is one of the few writers to refer to these musical changes. The following description of a performance in 1998 provides an insight into what Dylan was doing with this song at the time, and is a very good guide to what he does with many of his songs in concert:

> The current version of 'Tangled Up In Blue' begins, like the original one on *Blood on the Tracks*, with chiming major chords, but the onstage Dylan soon slips into a different scale – into the blues. Dismantling and rebuilding his own song piece by piece, he bends notes down, inverts the melody, spreads out the pitches of the chords, leans on a single note while the chords change around it, stresses the off beats, lays a triple rhythm on double ones. As the rest of the band holds on to straitlaced harmony and a one-two beat, the song tenses up: opposing scales meet in bittersweet clashes, opposing pulses overlap in a danceable bounce. At some point, the classic radio staple becomes a new animal. By the end, Dylan may be speaking right at you, but you're probably too caught up in the music to notice. (Ross 2004: 306)

Within months of releasing *Blood On The Tracks*, Dylan was shifting again, from introspective meditations on lost love and changed times to extroverted engagement with drama and spectacle, captured on the studio album *Desire* and *The Bootleg Series Vol. 5, Bob Dylan Live 1975, The Rolling Thunder Revue* and glimpsed in the film *Renaldo and Clara*.

The lyrics to all songs on *Desire* except 'Sara' and 'One More Cup Of Coffee' were co-written with theatre director Jacques Levy, who also helped to stage the Rolling Thunder Revue as a piece of music theatre rather than a conventional rock gig. The playwright Sam Shepard was also involved in staging this tour, and contributed ideas to the *Renaldo and Clara* film project. Dylan adopted his most theatrical stage manner during this period, appearing in white facepaint as a parodic inversion of blackface minstrelsy, using many dramatic arm and body gestures and at one performance taking to the stage wearing a Richard Nixon mask to deliver the first song, much to the initial confusion and then glee of the audience.

Musically Dylan began incorporating more varied textures and rhythms, using mandolin, bells and congas. One of the defining qualities of *Desire* is the large amount of reverb applied to the drums, in comparison to other instruments and voices, as if the drummer Howard Wyeth is in a huge cavern and the rest of the band are congregated at the entrance – an effect particularly noticeable on 'Isis' and 'Joey'. Crucial to Dylan's sound during this period was Scarlet Rivera's bluesy, gypsy-style violin (unlike the traditional fiddle-playing of folk and country) and the way she played off and with Dylan's harmonica, and the way Dylan's harmonica-playing often followed the violin. During 1975 performances were characterized by a light and delicate approach to acoustic songs and the ensemble numbers were often delivered as joyful, good-time boogies. Half-way through 1976, on the second Rolling Thunder tour, things had become more tense and strained, with reports of Dylan often being distraught, anecdotes about fraught domestic scenes, and stories of excessive drinking. The concert recorded towards the end of May 1976 and captured on *Hard Rain* features a performer who sounds emotionally strung out, delivering some of his most acerbic and emotionally intense performances on an album that (coincidentally rather than by design) seemed to resonate with the contemporary spirit of punk.

In 1978 Dylan undertook a major world tour of 115 shows in ten countries. According to various sources this was partly motivated by the need to raise cash after the losses incurred from his divorce settlement and the production costs not recouped from the film *Renaldo and Clara*. Dylan changed the texture of his band once again, augmenting guitars and keyboards with Steve Douglas on saxophone and flute, David Mansfield on mandolin and violin, and perhaps most significantly introducing female backing singers. The soulful, gospel-tinged vocals of Helena Springs, Jo Ann Harris and Carolyn Dennis developed and consolidated the sound Dylan had created when he incorporated female gospel vocals on *New Morning* and 'Knockin' On Heaven's Door'. Arrangements that integrated the drama of antiphony (call and response) allowed Dylan to give his songs a greater sense of social dialogue (an exchange between singer and others) and psychological tension (implying an internal dialogue with the singer's inner demons). This is immediately apparent from the first song on *Street Legal*, 'Changing Of The Guards'. The opening phrase "sixteen years" is echoed by the backing vocalists, who then introduce a recurrent tension into 'New Pony', with the relentlessly chanted "How much longer?" as an incessant voice (internal or external) that continually interrupts Dylan's blues.

Dylan had a specific sound in mind and told Robert Shelton: "I was determined that I was never gonna have the band sing anymore. It scatters their energy and they don't come up with the head sound I want, if they also sing" (1986: 477). Helena Springs also recalled that "he wanted girls that didn't sound like back-up singers, who had their own individual sound and just didn't blend" (1989: 71). Once introduced, the female vocalists would remain a frequent feature of Dylan's songs and live shows for the next ten years.

Dylan's songs on *Street Legal* are "peopled by a group of narrators who are oppressed, wandering, and lonely, travelling in a foreign country of the spirit" (Shelton 1986: 478). The songs delve into deceit, delusion and disillusionment through a poetic vocabulary that draws from metaphor, biblical allusion, myth, fable and blues poetry. With the exception of 'Señor (Tales Of Yankee Power)', which continued to appear in Dylan's live shows right up the end of 2006, and a rare one-off performance of 'We Better Talk This Over' in 2000, these songs were not performed live after 1978, suggesting that they have had little resonance for Dylan after this period.

The set performed on the early part of the 1978 tour was largely a "greatest hits" package, mainly owing to pressure from a Japanese promoter, but the attention given to song arrangements resulted in tight and polished performances from a large band. Apparently influenced by Neil Diamond's shows, this 1978 tour included make-up, glittery outfits, and some decorative big-band song arrangements that some US critics felt transformed Dylan's gigs into a Las Vegas-type show (the concerts didn't receive this response in Europe). Yet, for those of us into punk rock and post-punk music at the time, *Street Legal* seemed entirely relevant. Dylan was questioning and questing, dissatisfied and uncertain. Despite (or maybe because of) the big band, the record had a rough, dense and murky sound. Although some commentators have criticized its production (even when digitally remastered in the late 1990s), many who appreciated *Street Legal* at the time were embracing a recording aesthetic in which high production values were irrelevant, if not to be avoided. Dylan was connecting with a diverse range of people, drawing large audiences; the estimated 250,000 people who attended at Blackbushe Aerodrome in England in July was a clear indication of his popularity and relevance.

Saved but still searching

The introduction of gospel vocals along with *Street Legal*'s mood of emptiness and exile have in retrospect been interpreted as indicative of a deep spiritual yearning that caused Dylan to embrace evangelical Christianity and to make a very public display of his faith on *Slow Train Coming* and *Saved* and in a series of live shows during 1979 and 1980. There are fine instrumental performances, vibrant funky rhythms, uplifting horns, warm devotional organ-filled textures, memorable and unusual melodies and passionately expressive vocals on these albums, the tracks ranging from soulful ballads and funk-inflected blues to stark, sparsely arranged songs of praise and salvation. *Slow Train Coming* is one of Dylan's most slickly produced albums and *Saved* contains some of the most uplifting music he's ever made, the soulful title song being one of his most danceable tracks. Yet the instrumental and vocal performances and the varied musical textures are far more nuanced and subtle

© Peter Noble/Redferns

A gospel show, Toronto 1980

than Dylan's preoccupation with one overriding unambiguous lyrical theme. The lyrics, particularly on *Saved*, lacked the range of allusions that had characterized much of his music up to this point. Gone were the allegorical, figurative and symbolic subtleties of the preceding albums. It was impossible for fans to apply their own interpretation to the lyrics. There were no hidden meanings to be unearthed, no riddles to unravel.

If the content of these two albums posed a challenge to the audience, so too did the character of the live shows. From the autumn of 1979 through to May 1980, before releasing *Saved* in June, Dylan embarked on a gospel tour, giving concerts that did not include a single song that had been performed live before – no greatest hits, no nods to the glory days of the 1960s. Reviews and accounts from the time tell of energy and passion. They also tell a story of Dylan indulging in rambling apocalyptic rants, of people shouting at the stage, audience members arguing with each other, people walking out. The audience reactions at first were confused, mixed, and ambivalent. Although sporadic confrontations continued, within a couple of weeks the concerts were concluding with standing ovations as the audiences became familiar with the material and knew what to expect.

Many of the songs from *Slow Train Coming* and *Saved* were more dynamic live, with Dylan emphasizing their riffs and rhythms. 'In The Garden', for example, includes one of Dylan's most unusual melodies, hung on a sequence of rising chord changes that Allen Ginsberg had come up with when he and Dylan were out trick-or-treating (Trager 2004). In concert the song acquired a danceable quality as it became more riff-based, whilst retaining a sense of the narrative drama of the betrayal of Jesus Christ. 'In The Garden' became one of Dylan's most performed live songs of the 1980s and was still being played well into the 1990s, along with 'Gotta Serve Somebody', another song from this period.

By the time Dylan was touring again from the end of 1980 and into 1981 the Christian songs were gradually being dropped from the shows. The roots gospel feel continued into *Shot Of Love* (1981) but the sentiments became more secular – exemplified in the bluesy title track, which features one of Dylan's most impassioned vocal performances, a desperate plea for love that gains much of its power from the brilliant vocal interplay with Clydie King. *Shot Of Love* shows Dylan moving away from a preoccupation with Christianity, having taken from this experience an enhanced awareness of human frailty and mortality, a theme manifest in a series of elegiac songs that he wrote during the 1980s, starting with 'Every Grain Of Sand' and 'Lenny Bruce'.

Although Dylan continued to write songs in a range of styles, addressing different lyrical themes, his songwriting during the 1980s was pervaded by an introspective, slightly sombre and searching quality. There was little frivolity or wit. After *Shot Of Love* he appeared to be increasingly uncertain about the recording process. Biographers point to evidence of self-doubt and indecisiveness in the constant changing of producers, album mixes, recorded song arrangements, the increasing number of musicians used in different sessions and the quality of songs that were recorded but not released on albums at the time. *Infidels* (1983) often features in Dylan fan discussions as the album that *could* have been great – if only he'd included 'Blind Willie McTell', 'Lord Protect My Child' and 'Foot Of Pride'. Perhaps he might have added two songs that he'd left off *Shot Of Love*, 'Caribbean Wind' and 'Angelina'. 'Blind Willie McTell' combines remembrance of slavery with premonition of the apocalypse and has justifiably been recognized as one of Dylan's greatest songs. Yet he was unhappy with the piano and acoustic guitar demo with Mark Knopfler and a rather insipid band version. He eventually began performing a moody melodramatic version of the song live during 1997.

Dylan's anxieties and confusion about the changing methods of studio recording came to a head with the album *Knocked Out Loaded* (1986), which features over fifty musicians and vocalists recorded at numerous sessions, with instrumental and vocal textures that include trumpet, mandolin, congas, steel drums and children's choirs. On an album of just eight songs Dylan used six bass guitarists including James Jamerson Jr and Howie Epstein. Because of this, the album is confused, pulling in different directions even in the same song. The lone compensation is the epic eleven-minute cinematic 'Brownsville Girl', co-written with Sam Shepard. With its echoey, dense, wall-of-sound production and casual, semi-spoken vocal and dramatic interplay with the female backing vocalists, it is one of the few occasions when Dylan has constructed a sound world in the studio that probably couldn't be achieved in a similar way on stage. One line in the fictional narrative seemed to ring out and catch the ears of many critics: "If there's an original thought out there, I could use it right now." Ironic or desperate, or maybe both.

If Dylan had felt uncomfortable inside the rock circus without the elephants during 1974, he was even more out of place in the glossily packaged, video-promoted world of 1980s pop. Dylan also had many personal distractions, only some of which can be glimpsed in biographies. These included an ongoing business dispute with Albert Grossman that was not fully settled until after Grossman's death in 1986, and additional family commitments, notably a new wife and child.

Nowhere was Dylan's awkwardness more apparent than in the shambolic performance of 'Ballad Of Hollis Brown', 'When The Ship Comes In' and 'Blowin' In The Wind' with Ron Wood and Keith Richards at Live Aid in July 1985. Many factors could have contributed to the ramshackle performance including nerves, too much booze, no stage monitors to let the musicians hear what they were playing, considerable noise from behind the curtain at the rear of the stage and feedback through the PA system. On top of all this, Dylan broke a string during 'Blowin' In The Wind', and his only comment to an audience preoccupied with the plight of those living in the poorest parts of Africa was to suggest that some of the money could be used to help debt-stricken US farmers. It was yet another performance that upset people. This time it was many millions of television viewers.

Burlesque and biograph

Yet the very same year as Live Aid, in the midst of such apparent uncertainty and indecision, Columbia released two recordings that became central to the way Dylan would begin to find a new direction. The first was a collection of new songs released as *Empire Burlesque*. The second was a compilation box set with the title *Biograph*.

Critics who had followed Dylan since the 1960s were, and often still are, dismissive of *Empire Burlesque*. Just as *Nashville Skyline* was criticized because it was "country", so *Empire Burlesque* was rejected because it was "pop". As with the cover of *Nashville Skyline*, Dylan was ridiculed for his appearance. Gray calls him a "perplexed fashion-victim in Bruce Willis jacket" (2006: 209), the "dodgy" jacket apparently indicative of the music within.

Other commentators have recognized the value of this album. Shelton referred to it as "a major album, carefully produced, with free, excellent singing and an open expressionism in the soul vein" (1986: 492). It is one of Dylan's most carefully produced albums and includes some of his most emotive vocal performances, balanced with a varied palette of instrumental textures. The album condenses many of Dylan's influences, particularly early soul and gospel blues, and gives them a punchy contemporary pop sound with sax and horns, subtly ornamented with a touch of synthesizer or an inflection of bongo, the overall momentum acquiring a striking dynamism by the call and response, unison and harmony of female vocals.

Dylan clearly wanted to reach out beyond his older fans to a younger audience, and he employed Arthur Baker – a soul DJ and producer of hip-hop and dance music – to remix the initial tracks, adding a sharp brightness to the traditional rock blues timbre. Baker had remixed three of Bruce Springsteen's songs, 'Born In The USA', 'Cover Me' and 'Dancing In The Dark', from *Born In The USA* (released a year earlier), and Dylan was clearly impressed by the sound Springsteen had achieved on this album, along with the success that these remixes had brought him. Paul Williams has written favourably of *Empire Burlesque*, and I share his view that the decision to employ Baker to do the final mix was not only "unusual and daring", it was also "successful" (1992: 264). Once again Dylan was challenging those in his audience who were resistant to change whilst also testing himself as a musician. Perhaps the one aspect of production that stands out as "unnatural", dating the sound and disrupting the flow of the music, is the hissy, gated reverb that has been applied to the drums. The use of a "noise gate" creates a stuttering, staccato effect by simply cutting off the reverberation with an abrupt silence and not allowing the gradual decay to be heard (compare it with the decay of the reverb-laden drums on *Desire*, for example). This is very apparent on 'When The Night Comes Falling From The Sky'.

With *Empire Burlesque* Dylan began to introduce a more direct emotional language, less dependent upon complex imagery. Williams (1992) cites 'Emotionally Yours' as emblematic of how Dylan adopts a more direct way of addressing relationships, relying on the emotional resonance achieved through the delivery of a simple phrase rather than verbal cleverness and wordplay. John Hinchey also recognizes such depths and subtleties in the opening song, 'Tight Connection To My Heart (Has Anybody Seen My Love)' and writes of

> Dylan singing "Has anybody seen my love?" over and over in a tone that makes it sound like he's looking for some object he has mislaid, like an article of clothing or a book … With

each recurrence, however, the chorus grows less comic and
more poignant, as Dylan gradually relaxes his defences and
confronts the full reach of his despair. (1989: 56)

The directness of songs with familiar sentiments, allowing Dylan to find
poignancy in everyday phrases – in 'Seeing The Real You At Last', 'Trust
Yourself', 'Never Gonna Be The Same Again' – is finely offset against the
profound foreboding of 'When The Night Comes Falling From The Sky' and
the stark, underplayed 'Dark Eyes', a song given a brooding intensity when
performed as a duet with Patti Smith in Philadelphia during December 1995.

The significance of *Empire Burlesque* is not in the rare songs that have
endured beyond this period, but in how the album allowed Dylan to establish
a mood and an impulse that reached out towards a new type of audience
who were discovering his music for the first time. The other release of the
same year also allowed him to begin doing this.

The *Biograph* box set contains 53 tracks spread across five LPs or three
CDs and a detailed booklet containing previously unpublished photographs
and an interview in which Dylan candidly talked to Cameron Crowe about his
songs. It is one of the most significant Dylan releases of the 1980s, show-
casing thematically rather than chronologically a highly varied body of work,
displaying a range of different subjects, arrangements and voices, highlighting
just how difficult it is to pigeonhole Dylan. For new listeners it was an ideal
introduction to Bob Dylan, full of variety, depth, quirks and oddities. Yet it
also appealed to the long-time fan by including alternative versions of various
songs and previously unavailable recordings.

Biograph begins redefining the connections between Dylan's songs in
advance of his later touring, during which he would explore and develop
these realignments on stage. 'I Want You' (from *Blonde On Blonde*, 1966),
'Heart Of Mine' (from *Shot Of Love*, 1981) and 'On A Night Like This'
(from *Planet Waves*, 1974), for example, make sense musically and thematically alongside one another. They no longer need to belong to those albums
where they first appeared. It was an inspired and unusual release and the idea
of presenting Dylan's songs in this way seemed to grow in relevance over
the coming years. As with *Empire Burlesque*, the album reached out to a new
listener. Novelist Jonathan Lethem has written of how he became a fan during
this period and, distinguishing himself from those who grew up with Dylan

during the 1960s, he referred to himself as a member of "the Biograph generation ... the struggle to capture Dylan and his art like smoke in one particular bottle or another seemed laughable to me" (2006: 78).

During 1986 and 1987 Dylan toured with Tom Petty and the Heartbreakers, along with his backing vocalists, now called the Queens of Rhythm, performing many of the songs from *Empire Burlesque*. In the summer of 1987 he also played six stadium shows in the USA with the Grateful Dead (partly captured on the live album *Dylan & The Dead*). Although it is not very apparent on the live album, these concerts marked an important point when Dylan began to reassess how he was approaching performance. The Grateful Dead encouraged him to revisit songs from earlier years, particularly some of his less well-known numbers from the 1960s and 1970s; from this moment on, he began to perform songs that he hadn't played on stage before and to include a wider range of songs in future concerts. Dylan's experience with the Grateful Dead also caused him to reflect upon, or be reminded of, the way songs are realized on stage with an audience present, giving the performance a dynamism that is not usual present in the studio.

Dylan followed this with the Temples in Flames tour of September through October 1987 with Roger McGuinn and Tom Petty, taking to the stage with many musicians and subdued lighting, and playing songs that were beginning to sound overarranged, overplayed and occasionally cluttered. In May 1988, the album *Down In The Groove* was released, mostly a collection of cover versions, again featuring numerous musicians (about 30) and including tracks recorded over a six-year period. For many fans and critics this is Dylan's least inspiring collection of songs and performances. However, it does include 'Silvio', co-written with Robert Hunter, non-performing lyricist with the Grateful Dead, an underrated song, not well realized in the recording, but one that would later be given vibrant and joyful live performances (the same cannot be said for the other Dylan and Hunter collaboration, 'Ugliest Girl In The World' – a clumsily jokey song given a strangely ponderous production).

In *Chronicles: Volume One* Dylan is quite blunt about his artistic crisis in the mid- to late 1980s. He was asking himself three questions. The first concerned his performing identity: who was he now? Was he a relic of a bygone age? A nostalgia show? An artist that people paid to see simply to be in the presence of a legend? A second question concerned his songs:

© Ebet Roberts/Redferns

On stage with the Grateful Dead 1986

Dylan recalled that they had become "strangers" to him. He no longer knew what he was doing up on stage with them. The third question was about the audience, and he knew it was a problem. As he remembered: "I definitely needed a new audience" (Dylan 2004: 155). He wanted to find an audience that would not be too concerned with the past, as he also recalled in 1991: "It was important for me to come to the bottom of this legend thing, which has no reality at all. What's important isn't the legend, but the art, the work" (Heylin 2000: 666).

The road of renewal

Everything leads to the Never Ending Tour (NET). The phrase came from one of Dylan's quips to a journalist, a flippant remark that he subsequently distanced himself from in the liner notes to *World Gone Wrong*. But the label stuck with both fans and critics because it seemed to encapsulate Dylan's renewed approach to his life as a musician. All the songs, all the past experience of performing, all the weight and burden that had been heaped on his shoulders – the myth, the legend, the spokesman – everything came to a head during 1988 and coalesced into a straightforward answer to those questions about artistic identity, songs and audience.

Out go the large ensembles, out go the famous guest musicians, out go the backing vocalists, out go the lavish song arrangements that require planning and rehearsal. In comes a basic band – guitar, bass, drums – a few musicians who can respond on the night, a looser arrangement with greater opportunities for spontaneity. Out goes the idea of making albums and then doing tours. The tour is all there is; albums punctuate it (if there is the inclination to make them).

By constantly playing live Dylan sets out to find a new audience, seeking people without the old preconceptions and prejudices, people who will come out to the show and respond. Not people who will sit at home listening to the recording, immersed in nostalgia, and then attend an occasional show. There will now be a surfeit of shows. Out go the stadiums. Dylan makes a deliberate decision to play less-ostentatious venues, particularly in the United States, even if it means a residency of several nights in one place. He will no longer concentrate on the big cities but frequently play in smaller (often university or college) towns, with tickets priced to encourage the young and curious with nothing much to lose.

From this point on, the late summer of 1988, the albums will become increasingly less significant than the concerts – less relevant aesthetically (in terms of how Dylan's music is exposed and expressed) and less relevant as a means of communication (the way Dylan connects with the audience). The albums become the sideshow providing new material that might supply the main event – the live performance. They exist to feed the show, as do increasingly all Dylan's earlier compositions, along with numerous other songs, ranging from folk ballads and blues to songs by Leonard Cohen, Bruce Springsteen and the Beatles – some performed at only one show. The variety of set lists, the inclusion of unexpected numbers, the new arrangements, the subtle or major reinterpretations of repertoire become defining characteristics of Dylan as a musician from 1988 onwards. Lee Marshall's (2007) study of how Dylan's stardom was redefined by the Never Ending Tour gives some striking statistics about the live work. In the twenty-two years between 1966 and 1987 Dylan performed 534 shows, and there were a number of years (1967–73, 1977, 1982–3, 1985) when he didn't perform live or only made rare guest appearances with another artist. Between 1988 and 2006 he was on the road every year and played a total of 1913 gigs, an average of more than 100 shows a year.

With the NET he starts to play a far wider variety of songs live. He becomes less reliant on his most famous crowd-pleasers, those songs habitually applauded as they begin before anyone has even heard the performance. He introduces other crowd-pleasing songs, numbers that come over well live because they are clearly fun to play on stage, such as 'In The Garden' or 'Silvio' or 'Things Have Changed' or 'Thunder On The Mountain'. These songs might seem marginal as recordings but are persuasive and entertaining when performed at a crowded gig. Dylan also invents crowd-pleasing ways of delivering the old material. There is a noticeable shift in audience response. Although cheering, applause and vocal responses had begun to punctuate performances of his songs during the 1970s, the interjections now become more noticeable. A dialogue is created as listeners respond to a new arrangement or a particularly striking delivery of a familiar line. The songs are no longer a ritualistic celebration of a single history but become part of a continuing journey, one that draws new fans on the way.

As fans who have followed these shows would point out, there has not been one continuous tour, but rather a series of tours or a commitment to constant touring. Each year Dylan has usually been on the road from early spring (March/April) until around about Thanksgiving at the end of November, perhaps with a short summer break. He has frequently returned with new musicians after a break in live work, having changed song arrangements and with a different pool of songs to be used for a given section of touring. When critics write of Dylan changing set lists and song arrangements, they are referring less to significant changes in the musical structure and choice of songs to be performed from one night to the next and more to changes from year to year and over longer periods of time. At different stages of his touring he has adopted very specific and consistent arrangements and drawn each night's set list from an identifiable pool of songs.

The instrumentation of the touring band has also changed since 1988. During the early 1990s there were sections of the show when Dylan would play acoustic guitar alone. During the mid- to late 1990s the shows took on a harder electric blues timbre, with Dylan frequently playing electric guitar. From the late 1990s and into the new millennium there was a lighter folk and country feel, with acoustic guitars and upright bass augmented occasionally by fiddle, pedal steel and mandolin. From the autumn of 2002 Dylan began playing electric piano and during 2006 he switched the keyboard to an organ. Then, during 2007, the electric guitar reappeared for some boogie blues arrangements.

In some ways the NET poses a challenge to how the Bob Dylan story is told and how his music is defined, particularly for narratives led by chrono-logical discographies and detailed dissections of seemingly definitive album tracks. But in other respects it condenses and focuses a core that has always been evident from the beginning – the importance of the songs and the way Dylan performs them.

The author who has most persuasively put forward this view of Dylan is Paul Williams. Since way before Dylan embarked on this extensive touring, Williams has argued that one of the most significant characteristics of Dylan's art is the way he treats his songs as open to transformation and reinterpre-tation. It is a dynamic approach to both the songs and Dylan as an artist and it challenges those writers who want to fix and restrict the interpretation of Dylan's songs to a single or preferred meaning. Until recently it has been very difficult to evaluate or argue with such a position and there has been more than a suspicion that Williams's approach was imbued with the values of an in-crowd, the devoted élite who attend as many gigs as possible, the obsessive connoisseurs (with their collections of recordings and time to listen), who can then claim superior knowledge to those who only have access to the official albums and attended just a few gigs. Not so long back it did indeed take considerable effort and dedication to accumulate the material to support such an argument. But as music downloading and circu-lation on the internet has increased, and as sites have proliferated that have made available a range of unofficially recorded concerts, it has become possible for the novice Dylan follower to keep in touch with current live performances and to access an archive of audio recordings and visual images circulated by members of the audience. Inevitably, bootleg recordings will never capture the feel and atmosphere of being at a concert, but they give a pretty clear indication of how the performances sound and look.

Walking through the twilight into darkness

The album *Oh Mercy* (1989) benefits from Dylan's re-engagement with the spontaneous character of live music-making. Dylan had become dissatisfied with the way the studio had become an austere, clinical and dead environment during the 1980s. It was a confined space, accessed through corporate personnel and security, usually with no daylight, often with no natural reverberation, constrained by the intrusive presence of cables, amps, headphones, digital displays, buffers, booths or barriers separating the musicians. With more tracks available, musicians began routinely to record songs by playing their part alone, overdubbing in series rather than performing simultaneously as a dynamic ensemble. Dylan had often complained that his songs lost their vitality and character when recorded in this way or when performed too many times in this environment. Of performing live he later remarked, "Going onstage, seeing different people every night in a combustible way, that's a thrill. There's nothing in ordinary life that even comes close to that" (Muir 2001: 177). It is this "combustible" character of Dylan's music-making that has so often been lacking in the studio.

Daniel Lanois, the producer of *Oh Mercy*, was aware of Dylan's concerns. He had gained a reputation for creating a relaxed informal recording environment and made this album with portable equipment set up in different houses in New Orleans. Lyrically, the songs on *Oh Mercy* continued Dylan's fatalistic reflections on human foibles and conceits, thwarted dreams, and the painful memory of lost love, although he does allow the listener brief glimpses of hope and self-affirmation in 'Ring Them Bells', 'Most Of The Time', 'What Good Am I?' and 'Shooting Star'. Musically, the album has a skilfully blended mix of Dylan's relaxed singing, the lack of regular drum pulse in most tracks, and the creative application of echo, reverb and delay to the voices and instruments. The pivotal track is the gospel-tinged folk hymn 'Ring Them Bells', the song's lyrics echoed by sustained bell-like instrumental tones achieved with delay, repetition, and reverb. This ambience pervades the entire album and can be heard in the decaying piano chords, hanging suspended in mid-air before fading into the distance ('Ring Them Bells', 'What Good Am I?') and ringing guitars ('Where Teardrops Fall', 'What Was It You Wanted?', 'Most Of The Time').

Although *Oh Mercy* captures some outstanding performances, Lanois's approach to production was not inhibited by ideas of performative realism. Significantly in terms of Dylan's history, growing up being inspired by rhythm and blues and rock'n'roll, the sound on this album owed a debt to the echo and reverb techniques pioneered at Chess and Sun Records during the

1950s. Peter Doyle has written of the way echo allows the environment to answer back and "suggests at once the possibility of a deep, extended reciprocity between the self and the world, just as it indicates a total imprisonment in selfhood" (2004: 32). It is perhaps no coincidence that the lyrical themes of *Oh Mercy* frequently portray fraught encounters between absorbed self and volatile world ('Political World', 'Most Of The Time', 'Ring Them Bells', 'What Good Am I?', 'What Was It You Wanted?').

When echo and reverb were introduced on film soundtracks and in popular songs, particularly from the 1940s, they were used to convey a sense of twilight, a darkening of space, a dimming of light, or to give the impression of things losing their solidity as they blend into the surroundings, and to conjure up the presence of spirits, phantoms and mysteries (Doyle 2004). Echo and reverb were also used to evoke a dreamlike state, something that the Beatles made excessive use of in their mid-1960s recordings (*Sergeant Pepper's Lonely Hearts Club Band, Magical Mystery Tour*). Dylan had grown up during the same era as the Beatles and such sounds were undoubtedly part of his soundscape. Dylan was also influenced by 1950s blues and country records on which "echo and reverb effects were increasingly from this time onwards used to suggest shadowy, subterranean, marginal presences" (Doyle 2004: 39). All of these associations and sentiments seep deeply into *Oh Mercy*, where Dylan appears to inhabit a cavernous emptiness that echoes words, rhythms and notes. He drifts through a twilight world where phantoms of lost love or spectres of political demagoguery stalk past. On 'Man In The Long Black Coat', the production (beginning with the sound of crickets) evokes a gothic atmosphere of small-town paranoia, with intimations of supernatural presences and grotesque distortions of ordinary life. Dylan peers out from the shadows as a wailing harmonica sound echoes towards the edge of town, down deserted darkened streets. A stalking, unequalized bass underpins Dylan's hesitant, clipped vocal delivery. Seeming to be gasping for breath, placing accents on unexpected syllables, his singing encapsulates the mood of strangeness and unease.

Lanois's production allowed Dylan to synchronize and to play off musical and lyrical atmospheres, and this was repeated eight years later on *Time Out Of Mind*, Dylan's strongest collection of recorded songs since *Oh Mercy*. Again, much of the inspiration for the sound of *Time Out Of Mind* came from Dylan's dissatisfaction with the quality of contemporary recordings, and once more its production was informed by recordings made during the 1950s. Lanois first recorded musicians playing along with old recordings to try out arrangements and to make demos. He then integrated samples and loops from this into the mix. During the recording sessions Dylan and Lanois positioned musicians in the room and used strategically placed microphones to recreate the sonic perspective found on these old records. As a result, in many of the tracks the drums are way back in the mix, behind the other instruments, much like the production on Buddy Holly's recordings. *Time Out Of Mind* was mixed to emphasize the mid-range frequencies, with little at the top and bass end (again attempting to approximate a 1950s sound). The influence of Brian Eno's ambient production techniques is also apparent on this album, notably his habit of adding layers and treating sound in various ways. Lanois filled many gaps with drones, percussion, sustained guitar or organ chords.

If *Oh Mercy* resonates with the echoes of twilight, with glimpses of fading light, on *Time Out Of Mind* Dylan is in the darkness for much of the time, lyrically and musically, physically and spiritually. The hopelessness of broken love affairs, the loss of a person's presence, the persistence of memories, feelings of emptiness, are all amplified by an awareness of time passing – lost time that will never return, the little time left. Like many who need to reflect, or who simply have nothing better to do, Dylan takes to walking, connecting with and drawing from a long tradition of blues walkin' songs. The world appears to be closing in on Dylan, the thick dense textures and rhythms engulfing him as he tries to keep moving.

Time Out Of Mind contains some of the most unusual vocal treatments of any Dylan album. Overall, the voice has been equalized through various frequencies being boosted or reduced to exaggerate rather than downplay the raspy character of Dylan's voice. In addition, the vocal has been compressed; the contrasts between Dylan singing loudly and softly have been ironed out, making his softer singing sound unnaturally loud alongside the instruments. Throughout much of the album a very quick single "slap-back" echo has been added to the voice – a direct reference to the 1950s recordings of Elvis Presley. The most conspicuous treatment is the slightly flanged vocal on the opening track 'Love Sick', the compressed vocal and minimal echo giving Dylan's voice a constricted, alienated quality, sonically evoking his estrangement from lovers and friends (a theme in the album's lyrics).

The album was very well received. Dylan's contemporaries and reviewers were impressed by the way he was dealing with ageing and mortality in such bold and stark terms, singling out for praise the song 'Not Dark Yet', with its Dixie-style military drum rolls giving it a Civil War ballad feel. About half of the songs from the album have regularly featured in subsequent live shows.

Between these two inspired major albums was a typically Dylanesque mixture of playful wit and sardonic melancholia, and an approach to recording and performance that was more unpredictable than at any previous period. Joviality, self-deprecating humour and an occasional glint of musical satire were expressed as a member of the Traveling Wilburys (the others were George Harrison, Roy Orbison, Jeff Lynne and Tom Petty) on two albums (*Vol. 1* and *Vol. 3*) released in 1989 and 1990. Dylan's next solo album, *Under The Red Sky* (1990), included some good songs ('Under The Red Sky', 'Cat's In The Well') that were to be better realized in live performance than in this production by Don and David Was. Despite (or perhaps because) of the presence of star session players (Slash, Elton John, George Harrison, David Crosby, Stevie Ray Vaughan), the album presented a casually played, wishy-washy version of Dylan's mid-1960s sound. The inclusion of Al Kooper's swirling organ swells on this 1990 recording sounded strangely anachronistic and morosely nostalgic, particularly on 'Handy Dandy'. It gave an impression that Dylan was lethargically parodying Dylan (and maybe he was, on his time off from the Wilburys).

Live performances ranged from the unrehearsed and ramshackle to the focused and enthralling. During the winter of 1991 Dylan's singing was often incoherent, allegedly because he was drunk both off and on stage. Yet, in the autumn of the same year he played gigs that some critics rate as his best live performances. Many of his stage performances during 1995 and 1996 are still remembered as outstanding by those who attended, consistently characterized by riveting reinterpretations of his songs, a claim supported by bootleg recordings which present a very different singer from the one seen on MTV lethargically plodding through some of his best-known songs (*MTV Unplugged*, 1995) and from the nervous, thin, hesitant, reedy voice captured on *The 30th Anniversary Concert Celebration* (an all-star concert celebrating Dylan's thirty years in the music business, released by Columbia Records in 1993).

The two most significant albums from this period are *Good As I Been To You* (1992) and *World Gone Wrong* (1993). Recorded simply in Dylan's home studio, and featuring only voice, acoustic guitar and harmonica, the albums contain understated performances of traditional folk songs and rural blues, along with a version of 'Hard Times' by Stephen Foster. These albums are considered by some commentators to be significant artistic statements, Dylan realigning his public image with traditional songs and again refusing to acknowledge contemporary trends (Marshall 2007). Although complementing the traditional material that Dylan had been performing on tour, over half of the songs on these albums have never featured in Dylan's live shows, and his concerts have not featured a characteristic solo segment with just acoustic guitar and harmonica since the early 1990s. These two acoustic albums are not indicative of Dylan's instrumentation, arrangements and repertoire in concerts during this period. They do not logically follow from *Oh Mercy* or *Under The Red Sky*, and are not obvious precursors to *Time Out Of Mind*. Although some lyrics on *Time Out Of Mind* are sourced from traditional folk songs, the main inspiration for the production, songwriting and arrangements came from 1950s rhythm and blues and rock'n'roll. The albums follow each other in time, but once again Dylan's artistic decisions confound expectations and resist efforts to find any prevailing logic or overall pattern in the chronology.

Dylan had also been creating some country-tinged songs for film soundtracks, and at the beginning of the new millennium he received a Grammy for 'Things Have Changed', an evocative bluesy shuffle of social commentary and personal disillusionment. Created for the soundtrack of the 2000 film *The Wonder Boys*, it resulted in one of Dylan's best videos (perhaps inspired by the presence of Michael Douglas) and was to be regularly featured in his live sets.

Repeating the past

In 'Summer Days', the third track on *"Love And Theft"* (2001), Dylan deftly sings, "She says 'You can't repeat the past', I say 'You can't? What do you mean, you can't? Of course you can'." This dialogue, lifted almost verbatim from *The Great Gatsby* by F. Scott Fitzgerald, provides a theme that runs through Dylan's later songs on *"Love And Theft"* and *Modern Times* – taking songwriting inspiration from the undisguised appropriation and reuse of popular music from the 1930s to the 1950s, along with his perennial use of lyrics from old blues and ballads, and lines from poetry and novels. It is also a theme that threads through Dylan's other activities: writing a book of memoirs; hosting radio shows, during which he plays a huge number of songs recorded prior to the 1960s; and contributing droll observations on his early career to Martin Scorsese's documentary *No Direction Home* (2005).

"Love And Theft" is pervaded by wry humour, from the blend of nursery rhyme, nonsense verse and rockabilly pastiche on the opening 'Tweedle Dee & Tweedle Dum' through the self-deprecating jokes in 'Summer Days' (another rockabilly pastiche) and on to the clumsy puns and corny one-liners that he manages to croon deadpan on the fourth track, 'Bye And Bye' (a vaudeville pastiche). When it was released there could be little doubt that Dylan was enjoying the jokes, albeit with the usual moments of melancholia ('Mississippi') thrown in. Even 'Sugar Baby', the low-key and solemn final track (a characteristic feature of almost every Dylan album), is offset with some lightly sardonic lyrics. This is a very different world from the dim and bleak imagery evoked on *Oh Mercy* and *Time Out Of Mind*. The album also showed Dylan emphatically re-engaging with a direct, earthy, uplifting electric blues on 'Lonesome Day Blues' and paying tribute to acoustic Delta blues on 'High Water (For Charley Patton)'.

Modern Times (2006), five years later, begins in a similar mood, with the opening 12-bar blues shuffle 'Thunder On The Mountain', a sly shaggy-dog story in the spirit of 'Motorpsycho Nitemare' or 'Bob Dylan's 115th Dream', in which Dylan manages to search for soul singer Alicia Keys, recruit an army from orphanages and catch sight of "the ladies of Washington" desperately fleeing the panic-stricken city. Although the musical arrangements on *Modern Times* are generally lighter than on *"Love And Theft"*, the album journeys through bleaker scenery, notably on the slower songs. Dylan addresses a tender country waltz to a friend or lover who is about to die in 'When The Deal Goes Down'; nostalgically evokes the hardships of labour, along with human solidarity and camaraderie, in the haunting piano ballad 'Working Man's Blues #2'; and resolutely steps out into desolate, untended terrain in the final track, 'Ain't Talkin' ', yet another walking song. With slow ambling bass, soft droning strings, flickering picked guitar fading in and out, and a distant military snare, Dylan creates a sound reminiscent of the gothic sense of foreboding on 'Man In The Long Black Coat'. This time he's alone with his thoughts, grumbling in an ominous, low guttural voice about his pain ("walkin' with toothache in my heel") and the suffering of others, eventually finding that the gardener has gone. There is no hope, no salvation, only the emptiness and stillness of the "last outback at the world's end".

On *"Love And Theft"* and *Modern Times* there are no fancy attempts to recreate and incorporate 1950s production sounds, but 1950s musical styles and values are present in the instrumentation and clean and clipped guitar solos of Denny Freeman and Donnie Herron. Dylan takes producer's credit under his pseudonym of Jack Frost and settles for an unadorned live sound, using the musicians from his touring band and with little overdubbing. *Modern Times* opens with scattered chords, the sound of a group of musicians warming up, as if to say "this could be a bar band taking to the stage anywhere". Many of the songs on these albums, particularly the 12-bar blues, give the impression that they have been created for playing live, for entertaining the public, for having a good time during the never-ending touring – 'Lonesome Day Blues', 'Summer Days', 'Thunder On The Mountain', 'Rollin' And Tumblin' ' and 'The Levee's Gonna Break'.

"Love And Theft" marks a significant change in Dylan's approach to exposing the sources of inspiration for his songwriting. Rather than work on songs from elsewhere until they have been transformed and their origins camouflaged, the lyrical and musical debts are piled up and openly paraded. The album title deliberately or coincidentally adopts the phrase used by Eric Lott in his 1993 scholarly study of blackface minstrelsy. Dylan puts inverted commas around it – just to make his theme and method even more obvious. A plethora of riffs, lyrics and melodies that have their origins in other songs and writings are included in an unconcealed manner, taking in the inevitable lines from old blues songs with more unusual borrowings, such as the storyline of *Confessions of a Yakuza* by Junichi Saga. The blatant use of existing tunes, poetry and lyrics continued on *Modern Times*, with Dylan lifting words, melodies, arrangements from blues shuffles, folk, pre-rock'n'roll pop and the nineteenth-century poetry of Henry Timrod. Within days of each album's release fans were circulating lists of the songs' sources. Speaking to journalists after *"Love And Theft"* was released, Dylan told of a box in which he kept quotations, phrases and lines of text. When asked about particular songs on this album, he commented, "The box wrote that" (Barker 2005: 316).

Modern Times was to become one of Dylan's most commercially successful albums, released at a time when his profile in the media was higher than
it had been for years, as a result of a major documentary film, radio series
and book. The film, *No Direction Home*, directed by Martin Scorsese,
which narrated Dylan's musical career from childhood until 1966, was shown
on television around the world during 2005 and introduced Dylan's earlier
music to a new generation unaware of his significance, his musical and visual
style, and the controversy he provoked between 1964 and 1966. Dylan's
book of memoirs, *Chronicles: Volume One*, was published towards the end
of 2004 and was unanimously praised by literary critics and book reviewers.
Bob Dylan's Theme Time Radio Hour, broadcast over various radio networks
and via the internet during 2006 and into 2007, allowed listeners to hear
the wry, deadpan, jokey, gnarled voice behind the ironic songs on *"Love And
Theft"* and *Modern Times*. These albums, along with *Theme Time Radio
Hour*, encapsulated Dylan's approach to his identity and music in the new
millennium – reinvestigating the songs that inspired him in the 1940s and
1950s and returning to a mixture of the profound and frivolous, the comic
and the caustic, that he explored so successfully during the first half of the
1960s.

With Dylan's media profile so high, a number of the students I was
teaching in London discovered him for the first time after seeing *No Direction Home*. One had bought his first Dylan album, *No Direction Home: The
Soundtrack. The Bootleg Series Vol. 7*. His initial serious engagement with
Dylan's songs thus involved listening to various out-takes, live versions and
alternative takes. He was getting the songs but not the "original" versions
that were so familiar to and almost taken for granted by many older fans. He
asked me what to listen to next and it seemed to me that the most logical
next step would be *Biograph*, for the way it too provides different versions,
but also for the way it challenges Scorsese's narrative, argument and period
emphasis (not that he needed, or would necessarily follow, my suggestion
anyway). Yet another new, young fan was discovering Dylan, beginning to
chart his own course through the songs, just as many others have been doing
for nearly fifty years.

For many critics who grew up listening to Dylan from the early 1960s,
his songs may be irredeemably linked to particular albums. But they are not
frozen in time. As recorded artefacts they continue to circulate and connect

with new fans in different circumstances, while the songs in concert are drawn from a repertoire that dissolves the arbitrary distinction between one album and another, making it permeable and irrelevant. The songs are continually finding new resonances, acquiring further meanings, linking up with songs from elsewhere. This is not only due to the digital networks allowed by the internet, but directed by the way Dylan himself has been continually defining new relationships *between* his songs in his shows over the years. By the mid-2000s Dylan was able to draw from a repertoire of songs that he had written and recorded over a forty-five-year period. To tell the story of Dylan as a musician in terms of albums would leave 'Masters Of War' and 'Blowing In The Wind' as acoustic tracks in the early 1960s, 'Tangled Up In Blue' in its mid-1970s guise, and 'Cold Irons Bound' with Daniel Lanois's "swampy" production in 1997. By 2007 'Highway 61 Revisited' had become almost wholly detached from its 1965 appearance as surreal stream of consciousness. Instead, it had become a good-time r'n'b boogie performed alongside the rockabilly irreverence of 'Summer Days', the bluesy nursery-rhyme innuendo of 'Cat's In The Well', and the wry laid-back rock'n'roll shuffle of 'Thunder On The Mountain'.

To present a linear artistic chronology can be misleading, but signalling the continuities, changes, cyclical turns and seemingly paradoxical twists is not easy. This chapter has inevitably been broad-ranging and selective. I hope I have not implied too much unity, continuity and closure, because there is always going to be something more to say, to notice, and to hear. There will always be some other way of interpreting and ordering the Bob Dylan songbook.

3 Traditions

Like many great songwriters, Bob Dylan has been able to draw influence and find inspiration by closely following an existing tune, lyrical theme or chord sequence while transforming it, making it anew, breathing new life into established forms. Dylan's music is firmly embedded within specific popular song, blues and ballad traditions, and many of his compositions are quite deliberately constructed from existing elements. Although his recordings have often been appreciated according to the criteria of rock criticism, with its emphasis on the apparent originality of musicians who write their own songs, Dylan has always followed a songwriting philosophy drawn from folk music, working with and reusing existing songs, forms and styles. Yet the borrowed musical and lyrical phrases, the stolen riffs and the hooks are edited, remade and intensely personalized. Robert Christgau alluded to this in an overview of the music of 1997, the year when *Time Out Of Mind* was released, commenting that the apparent "timelessness" that people hear in Dylan's music "is what Dylan has long aimed for – simple songs inhabited with an assurance that makes them seem classic rather than received" (1998, np). It has been Dylan's creative use of existing musical materials that has so often given his songs their "classic" (rather than received) character.

A second point follows from Christgau's observations and it concerns the way Dylan *inhabits* his and other songs. He gets inside them. He opens them up and sings them from within. In *Chronicles: Volume One* he remembers the impact of hearing Kurt Weill and Bertolt Brecht's song 'Pirate Jenny' and writes of "taking the song apart, trying to find out what made it tick" (2004: 275). This is an analytical trait of great singers, whether Bessie Smith or Billie Holiday, Frank Sinatra or Maria Callas; each occupied the song, lived it as they sang it. It is also the mark of great songwriters to get inside the song as form, to understand what makes it work musically, and to inhabit the song as lyric, to understand the perspective from which it is being sung. Paul Williams made a related point when listening to a recording of Dylan performing in 1960, before he went to New York, and hearing how the voice "shapes itself to the rhythm and character of each different song. It is as though he's trying to become the song" (1990: 14).

This chapter is about the most significant musical traditions through which Dylan has moved, the sounds he has inhabited and used to shape his songs – blues, country and folk. I start, however, with a brief detour through the legacies of childhood.

Nursery rhymes and fairy tales

At a very young age children learn about melody and rhythm through commercial pop songs, popular tunes and nursery rhymes. In Iona and Peter Opie's introduction to *The Oxford Dictionary of Nursery Rhymes* they remark, "It's probably a fact that every one of us could recite a string of nursery rhymes before we knew the meaning of the words which form them" (1997: 42). From our earliest days we take pleasure from the sensual appeal of sung words as sounds before we can understand them or even quite regardless of what they might mean as semantic statements. As young children we learn that understanding and communicating in the world is about sound, gesture, touch, texture and colour. When children start laughing and finding things funny, it is often because of the sound (rather than the meaning) of a word. When children start singing, they take pleasure in making sounds and rhythmically repeating them, often seemingly endlessly, to the irritation of some adults. This is just one of the legacies of nursery rhymes, a thread that weaves throughout popular music and one of the sources of pleasure for musicians and listeners.

Many of the nursery rhymes that we still encounter were not written for children in the first place. They were popular songs, slogans, satires, chants, riddles, street cries, and bits of ballads that eventually found their way *into* the nursery, as it became an institution associated with the modern notion of childhood during the nineteenth century, and as the child became viewed as a person distinct from the adult. Michael Gray's study of Dylan credits children as the "curators" of folk song traditions, arguing that we should value nursery rhymes not as a historical record of their times but for "their poetry, their vivacity, their energy of character, story and language, and in the democratic, communal process (the oral tradition …) that invents them and keeps them alive" (2000: 639).

When Dylan released *Under The Red Sky* in 1990, the nursery rhyme references were explicit, and Gray calculated that this album "makes direct raids on thirty-two nursery rhymes and game songs, and offers demonstrable correspondences with three fairy tales and a further fifteen nursery rhymes" (*ibid.*: 701). Gray has explored in detail the way Dylan has performed songs associated with the nursery, from the 'The Cuckoo Is A Pretty Bird' in 1961 to 'Froggie Went A-Courtin'' in 1993 and has continually used "nursery rhyme formulae" in his songwriting.

Nursery-rhyme influences run throughout the history of the blues, and inevitably feed from this into rock'n'roll. They can be found in Blind Willie McTell songs, overtly in Leadbelly's children's songs, in Chuck Berry – the notable "hey diddle diddle" in 'Roll Over Beethoven' – and Bo Diddley's 'Nursery Rhyme'. The use of nursery rhyme in blues allowed songs to communicate in different ways to adults and children, most notably through the use of sexual *double entendre* in the recurrent references to pussies, cats, dogs, toads and frogs (for example, Jane Lucas and Big Bill Broonzy's 'Pussy Cat Blues'). Dylan used the typical blues mixture of nursery innocence and sexual innuendo in 'Cat's In The Well'.

Nursery-rhymes allow songwriters opportunities for a poetics of trickery and game-playing. Sometimes Dylan has used nursery rhyme formulae explicitly, as in 'Who Killed Davey Moore?' ('Who Killed Cock Robin?') and the jokey 'I Shall Be Free No. 10', with its use of children's counting songs, along with the "fee fi fo fum" from Jack and the Beanstalk and "I don't know but I've been told, the streets of heaven are lined with gold" (more or less the same line that Dylan had sung in 'Gospel Plow' on his first album). On other occasions it has been more subtle. Gray highlights how 'A Hard Rain's A-Gonna Fall' draws on the folk ballad 'Lord Randall', a song that had largely been preserved orally as a nursery rhyme. It also echoes imagery in other nursery rhymes (such as "six crooked highways"). Paul Williams argues that the meaning of 'A Hard Rain's A-Gonna Fall' is largely conveyed through a structure that is indebted to "a form similar to a nursery rhyme or a recital in school" (1990: 59). 'Scarborough Fair', a song that Dylan drew on lyrically and melodically for 'Girl From The North Country', is a narrative that had been handed on as a form of both fairy tale and nursery rhyme. Indeed, it is the echoes of nursery rhymes – submerged or camouflaged – rather than their explicit use that is most pervasive in Dylan's songs. Gray finds these echoes in 'With God On Our Side', 'Boots Of Spanish Leather', 'Ballad In Plain D', 'Restless Farewell', even in 'Desolation Row' and later songs such as 'When Teardrops Fall' and 'Highlands'. Many writers have commented upon the nursery rhyme influences apparent on the *Basement Tapes* (Dylan had a young family at the time), and Dylan himself called 'The Mighty Quinn' a nursery rhyme (Crowe 1985). As so many have noticed, one of Dylan's best-known songs, 'Like A Rolling Stone', begins with the anticipatory prelude to fairy tales "Once upon a time ...".

Dylan is not alone in using fairy tale and nursery rhyme imagery in the popular song. His 1960s contemporaries the Beatles littered their songs with nursery rhyme quotations, nursery rhyme language, fairy-tale imagery, and characters that would be quite at home in the nursery – a few of the more obvious songs being 'Yellow Submarine', 'All Together Now', 'Cry Baby Cry' and 'Mean Mr Mustard'. Childhood references permeated the Beatles' songs, from jokey word games and fun with rhyme ('Mean Mr Mustard', 'I Am The Walrus') to the more profound ways that they conveyed lost innocence ('Strawberry Fields', 'Golden Slumbers'). When McCartney's solo record 'Give Ireland Back To The Irish' was banned from being mentioned, let alone played, on British radio in 1972 he retorted by releasing 'Mary Had A Little Lamb'.

There are three significant ways that Dylan and the Beatles drew from nursery rhymes. First, there was the way these seemingly simple childhood ditties provide opportunities for verbal trickery, allowing songwriters to have fun with the sound of words as they play with rhyme and rhythm. Nursery rhymes are highly rhythmic, melodically familiar and adaptable. Second, in a deceptively condensed way nursery rhymes manage to blend ethical and emotional wisdom with a touch of the fantastic and mysterious. They can be used to convey an almost mythical moral wisdom, to impart concisely a sense of good and evil. Third, they attune us to the pleasures and the power of apparently simple melodies and chants, a point I shall return to in Chapter 5.

The blues

The blues is one of the most important influences on Dylan's music. It is there in the sound of his voice – the nasal timbre, the stretching and extending of phrases, in his use of breathing and adoption of an ordinary voice that becomes extraordinary in song. As Gunter Schuller once noted when discussing the blues voice,

> Ma Rainey's recordings expose clearly what is intrinsic to the blues; not a "cultured" vocal delivery, but an individual expressiveness, where word, meaning, and sound are all one. The beauty of the blues, as sung by Ma Rainey or Bessie, is that it is at once as natural as everyday speech and yet an individualized artistic expression. (1968: 228)

Schuller has also written of Bessie Smith's "unique ability to break phrases into unexpected segments and to breathe at such phrase interruptions without in the slightest impairing over-all continuity, textual or melodic" (*ibid.*: 233). Such characteristics can be found in so many of the other blues singers who have influenced Dylan, particularly Charley Patton, Robert Johnson, Son House and Bukka White.

The blues can be heard in the way Dylan's melodies slide across and between notes, the way he flattens certain notes of the conventional major and minor scales. It is sometimes said that there is a blues scale or blues mode that can be played by most obviously flattening the third and the seventh, and also the fifth and sixth notes of a scale. However, studies of early Delta blues recordings and later electric blues have shown quite clearly that all twelve pitches of the conventional western chromatic scale may be flattened, bent or altered in some way during performance (Titon 1994; Weisethaunet 2001). These flattened notes are sometimes called "blue notes", although this term is derived from western musicology, based on classical notation, and used as a way of categorizing and ordering notes that don't seem to conform to "the rules". If you've grown up listening to blues, folk, jazz, early rock (prior to the obsessive auto-tuning of voices and instruments), you'll be almost instinctively familiar with these "microtonal" fluctuations, the way singers and instrumentalists bend and slide between notes. Dylan has immersed himself in folk and blues traditions where performers sing far more pitches than could easily be recorded by the limited conventions of European notation, based on the twelve semitones within an octave. To borrow a phrase that has been used a number of times when referring to the blues tradition, Dylan sings across the cracks between the notes on the piano. Like so many blues singers, he frequently sings melodic lines that, from the perspective of the "rules" of European classical harmony, are not rooted in or directly related to notes contained within the underlying chords.

The blues can be heard in the stark acoustic guitar strumming, stabbing or picking. It can be heard in the way Dylan and his musicians use instruments to subvert their apparently fixed pitches – bending the pitch of notes, slightly lowering the pitch of strings to add timbric colour and harmonic overtones. Inevitably, it is easier to bend notes on some instruments than others; it is easier to slide down or up with the voice, the guitar, the violin or the trombone. It is harder on the harmonica, although the pitch can be bent by changing the embouchure (the shape of the mouth on the instrument) or by blowing harder or softer. Dylan became adept at achieving various blues harmonica effects, ranging from the lonesome mournful wail where notes are left suspended and moaning in space, through joyous rhythmic train-like chugging influenced by Jesse Fuller, along with Jimmy Reed's style of bending notes as he blew out and the distinctive staccato playing of Sonny Terry.

The spirit of the blues can be heard in Dylan's reliance on subtle fluctuations across the apparently "simple" and repetitive chord sequences that make the blues so compelling and exciting. He draws on a blues that can be played on one chord ('Political World', 'T.V. Talkin' Song'), or with a brief fluctuation to a second chord ('New Pony', '10,000 Men', 'High Water (For Charley Patton'). He makes extensive use of a blues that can be improvised around what is known as the three-chord 12-bar blues. Most blues players don't think with notions of "bars", and if transcribed according to conventional notation a sequence may seem to be an irregular combination of 13-bar or 15-bar or 12-and-a-half-bar blues or various similar permutations. The 12-bar blues refers to a pattern, used time and time again, which entails a shift from a "root" chord of I, up to the fourth (IV), back to the root (I), and then visiting the fifth chord (V) and maybe the fourth (IV) on the way back to the root (I). In the key of C, this would involve a journey to chords based on C(I), F(IV), C(I), G(V), F(IV). If you are not a musician, you can work out what this chord sequence sounds like by listening for the shifts in pitch and return to previously heard chords. Or you can get hold of a guitar, get a chart showing you basic chord patterns (E, A, B7 or C, F, G7), put your fingers on the frets, hold down the strings and strum. It will take you less than an hour and you'll begin to hear a basic blues.

These blues chords (identified as I, IV or V) do not conform to the conventional western art music notions of major and minor scales and chords (and all the naïve assumptions about brightness and sadness that go with the major/ minor dichotomy). From the classical perspective of hearing pitches, music that works with the blues will contain so-called "dissonances". Songs will often appear to simultaneously contain the third note of the scale as both "natural" and flattened (of course, musicians and fans don't hear these as "dissonant"). Some of Dylan's blues might be heard as leaning towards minor chords ('Million Miles'), others may appear to lean towards the major ('Thunder On The Mountain'), but the sonic texture can't be collapsed or abstracted into this narrow way of representing music. When Dylan does base a song on "one" chord, it is often far from easy to work out the exact notes that make up the chord and how they drop in, drop out or become drones throughout a particular song (to think that a blues is "simply" on one chord is also to ignore everything else that is going on), the verses of 'Cold Irons Bound' being a good example here. In addition, Dylan's bands, like many blues musicians, may occasionally appear to play notes from the fourth (IV) and the fifth (V) chord simultaneously, or the fourth and the fifth may be bent into each other, something that happens in a lot of blues, gospel and jazz. This creates tension, anticipation and dynamism, propels the songs forward and is not difficult for any musician to do. Some of this might look rather frightening on sheet music if transcribed (it may sound scary here), but these aspects are rarely notated. The sheet music of Dylan's songs that appears in songbooks is, in general, very simplified, schematic, often misleading and frequently notated in a key he has used neither live nor in the studio. Look in a Dylan songbook and you'll see lots of basic triad chord shapes: listen to albums and live recordings and you'll hear a whole lot more notes.

The 12-bar blues pattern is particularly noticeable in Dylan's songs from the earliest days of his rural folksy blues ('Down The Highway', 'Black Crow Blues', 'Outlaw Blues', 'On The Road Again', 'Bob Dylan's 115th Dream') through the amplified, Chicago style that went with the surreal stream-of-consciousness quality of his mid-1960s songs ('Highway 61 Revisited', 'Just Like Tom Thumb's Blues', 'Leopard-Skin Pill-Box Hat', 'Obviously Five Believers'). This pattern is not so prominent during a period from the late 1960s through to the early 1990s, when he is composing more clearly structured narrative songs and experimenting with different tunings (*Blood On*

The Tracks), using varied sound textures (*Desire, Street Legal, Oh Mercy*), embracing gospel (*Slow Train Coming*), and trying to achieve a sound influenced by mainstream pop and rock styles (*Infidels, Empire Burlesque, Under The Red Sky*). Yet the 12-bar blues pattern is there throughout this period in such songs as 'Meet Me In The Morning', 'Gonna Change My Way Of Thinking', 'Groom's Still Waiting At The Altar', 'Man Of Peace', 'Ugliest Girl In The World', 'Everything Is Broken', 'Unbelievable' and 'Cat's In The Well'. The Never Ending Tour seems to encourage its re-emergence in Dylan's performances during the 1990s and the three-chord blues pattern returns as a prominent feature with *Time Out Of Mind* ('Dirt Road Blues', 'Million Miles', 'Till I Fell In Love With You', 'Can't Wait', 'Highlands'), continuing with *"Love And Theft"* ('Summer Days', 'Lonesome Day Blues', 'Honest With Me', 'Cry A While') and *Modern Times* ('Thunder On The Mountain', 'Rollin' And Tumblin'', 'Someday Baby', 'The Levee's Gonna Break').

Dylan's recollections of how Robert Johnson made his "hair stand up" (2004: 282) give a compelling insight into how the blues have influenced his manner of writing and delivering a song: "The stabbing sounds from the guitar could almost break a window. When Johnson started singing, he

On stage with the Band 1974

seemed like a guy who could have sprung from the head of Zeus in full armour" (*ibid.*). Dylan writes of how he spent weeks listening to the songs over and over again, thinking about how Johnson mixed musical economy with rhythmic sophistication. As he recalled:

> I copied Johnson's words down on scraps of paper so I could more closely examine the lyrics and the patterns, the con- struction of his old-style lines and the free association that he used, the sparkling allegories, big-ass truths wrapped in the hard shell of nonsensical abstraction – themes that flew through the air with the greatest of ease. I didn't have any of these dreams or thoughts but I was going to acquire them. (*ibid.*: 285)

Dylan's lyrics are infused with rhymes, rhythms and imagery drawn from the blues. Johnson influenced how he began to use words for both literal and metaphorical associations. As Peter Guralnick has written:

> Whereas someone like Son House or Charley Patton was content to throw together a collection of relatively traditional lyrics, known as "floating verses," which, however effective their emotional impact or even their story-telling specifics, never fully achieved thematic coherence, Johnson intentionally developed themes in his songs; each song made a statement, both metaphorical and real. (1989: 37)

Dylan absorbed Johnson's real and metaphorical imagery, often directly quot- ing him. The image of "blues fallin' down like hail" in Johnson's spooky 'Hellhound On My Trail' is more or less directly quoted in 'Nettie Moore'; the phrase "killin' me by degrees" from 'Preaching Blues' is sung by Dylan in 'Where Are You Tonight?'

Some writers have viewed Dylan's songs as a rewriting and resignifying of the blues, adding an apparently more knowing, sophisticated and arty point of reference. But there was only a brief period (1965–66) when he was grafting surreal, absurd and grotesque imagery onto blues patterns, and the lyrics from this moment have often been overanalysed, detracting from the way Dylan has used a vernacular language of the blues throughout his musical life. Like all blues singers, he has directly quoted by using melodies, phrases, couplets or titles from existing songs. For example, 'New Pony' from *Street Legal* draws on the lyrics of Son House's 'The Pony Blues' and Charley Patton's 'Pony Blues' and from other songs with the same theme. Dylan has explicitly acknowledged his debt to Charley Patton in 'High Water (For Charley Patton)' from *"Love And Theft"*, drawing on songs that comment on the Mississippi flood of 1927, including Patton's 'High Water Everywhere' and Blind Lemon Jefferson's 'Rising High Water Blues', from which Dylan takes the opening phrase "High water risin'".

Dylan has taken lyrics from numerous songs. 'Lay, Lady, Lay' owes a debt to Ruth Willis and Blind Willie McTell's 'Rough Alley Blues', in which they sing "lay you across my big brass bed". The extensive references to walking on *Time Out Of Mind* draw on a blues tradition exemplified by Ma Rainey's 'Walking Blues', in which she sings about continual walking and lack of time – two of the main themes of Dylan's album. Many of the songs on both *"Love And Theft"* and *Modern Times* explicitly use blues for inspiration. Michael Taft has compiled a valuable anthology of *Blues Lyric Poetry* (1983). On the first page this reprints two lyrics: 'Long Lonesome Day Blues' by Texas Alexander, recorded in 1927, which begins "Yes, today has been a long old lonesome day" – almost identical to the first line of 'Lonesome Day Blues'; and 'Dough Roller Blues' by Garfield Akers, recorded in 1930, which begins "I rolled and I tumbled and I cried the whole night long" – identical to the first line of 'Rollin' And Tumblin'' and many blues with the same theme or title. Dylan has also used existing titles, such as 'Tombstone Blues' or 'Sugar Baby', even though his songs do not musically resemble their name-sakes. In fact, "blues" is one of the most recurrent words in Dylan's song titles.

Dylan's songs are pervaded with blues imagery drawn from the landscape of the Mississippi Delta – the river, the floods, the levee, the lowlands – as well as various stock phrases from the blues ("woke up this morning", "jump and shout", "rollin' and tumbling'"). Dylan's portrayal of women in songs also owes a huge debt to the blues, particularly the recurrent themes of being deceived and mistreated. Although women are outnumbered by men in the histories of blues, the conventions have always allowed women to complain about their men and men to complain about their women. Bessie Smith or Memphis Minnie could sing of the way men made them despair, provoked defiance or drove them into seeking revenge. Ma Rainey sang "trust no man no further than your eyes can see". On *"Love And Theft"* Dylan sang "there ain't no limit to the amount of trouble women bring" in 'Sugar Baby'. Delivered in 2001, amid other jokey lines on this album, Dylan's lyric sounds less like a heartfelt remark and more like an ironically lifted phrase that parodies the male blues sigh.

In tracing the influence of the blues on Dylan's lyrics it is wise not to get too bogged down in the poetry of the blues and heed the words of Albert Murray:

> As compelling as so many blues lyrics so often are, and for all the apt phrases, insightful folksay, and striking imagery that blues singers have added to the national lore, the definitive element of a blues statement is not verbal. Words as such, however well chosen, are secondary to the music. What counts for most is not verbal precision (which is not to say vocal precision) but musical precision, or perhaps better still, musical nuance. Even the most casual survey of the recordings of Ma Rainey, Bessie Smith, Louis Armstrong, Jimmy Rushing and Big Joe Turner, to say nothing of Blind Lemon Jefferson, Leadbelly, and Robert Johnson, will show that it is not at all unusual for blues lyrics of the very highest poetic quality to be mumbled, hummed, and even garbled by the outstanding performers of the idiom. (2000: 79)

The blues had a profound and enduring impact on Bob Dylan, as they did on many musicians and listeners of his generation. Dylan acquired a means of expression from the blues voice, from the musical matrices of the blues, and from the language of blues lyric poetry. He incorporated and absorbed the idiom and style into his musical identity and over time it has become clear that Dylan is far more part of a blues tradition than any modern-day rock tradition.

Country

As a teenager during the 1950s much of the music that Dylan heard on the radio was country music. The musical roots of country, like the blues, are in the south of the United States, where ballad forms from Europe met the music and rhythms of Africa. Immigrants from Europe had brought guitars;

slaves from West Africa had brought an early version of the banjo (although they were often forbidden from playing percussion, the banjo frequently escaped sanction). Through a complicated pattern of musical exchanges and dialogues, the banjo eventually became more associated with country (and blackface minstrelsy) as a "white" music and the guitar became central to the blues as a "black" music. British and Irish ballads, Christian hymns, African-Arabic influenced vocal styles and rhythms were absorbed into the two traditions that became known as blues and country music. Yodelling, too, was a feature of early blues and country, prominent in the performances of Jimmie Rodgers, who recorded from 1927 until his early death in 1933 and who has been called "the father of country music" and a "white blues singer". In the early part of the twentieth century many singers, whether performing in and around the Mississippi Delta or in the Appalachian mountain region, would play vaudeville numbers, popular tunes of the day, along with old ballads. As they did this, they bridged and confused the divisions that now separate recordings into blues, country and folk. You can hear the blues in the bent notes and railroad imagery of Jimmie Rodgers; you can hear country in the hillbilly struts and mournful pleas of Blind Willie McTell.

The separation of music and musicians into identifiable genres had more to do with the social divisions of race and less to do with straight musical differences. It had a lot to do with the marketing decisions of the entrepreneurs (such as Henry Speir or Ralph Peer) who made records. Jimmie Rodgers was initially categorized as a "hillbilly" singer and was sold to white folks, whereas blues singers were sold on "race recordings" to black folks. The divisions were reinforced by the geographical fragmentation of cities, the separation of populations in the countryside and neighbourhoods, and most perniciously through laws that kept white and black people apart in public places, schools and employment. Yet, when teenagers like Robert Zimmerman were listening to their radios up in Hibbing during the early 1950s, the blues and country music coming over the airwaves was arriving without the appearance of the singer.

During the early years of recording, the music that would become country was sometimes labelled as "old-time music" or "hillbilly", the latter a pejorative term to designate someone who was unschooled, rough, simpleminded and from the backwoods of the Appalachian Mountains (Peterson

1997). Even the more neutral term "country" (or "country and western") that was introduced during the mid-1940s has been treated suspiciously by those anxious about its enduring association with bigotry and racism. Reflecting on this point, country music historian Bill C. Malone observed that "Southern intellectuals, particularly Southern liberal intellectuals, have been very embarrassed by the music" (Tichi 2005: 353).

If Southern intellectuals have been embarrassed, those in the Northern states and Europe have often been highly dismissive of country. Many a writer has concurred with Simon Frith's sweeping generalization that country music is a "conservative form carrying a conservative message" (1983: 24–5). It is for these reasons that many left and liberal intellectuals have felt uncomfortable about Dylan's engagement with country music.

One response to such a position is to argue that country music cannot be reduced to such a simple caricature. Although it has often appeared to be aligned with the Republican party, and been endorsed by its politicians, country has also been made by maverick performers with roots in white working-class radicalism, cultural populism and evangelical Protestantism (Lipsitz 1990) – a historical legacy that led to the sub-genre of alt-country or Americana. Many of Dylan's influences are in this line, and indeed Woody Guthrie was labelled as a hillbilly when he was performing radical populist songs during the 1930s.

Yet the issue is not entirely straightforward. Some critics have challenged the view of Dylan as a radical, left-leaning figure. For example, focusing mainly on Dylan's use of Christian imagery and generalizing from the brief moment when he embraced a "religious framework for his beliefs" (Webb 2006: 59), Stephen Webb has argued of the period from *Highway 61 Revisited* in 1965 to *Saved* in 1980: "Dylan embodied the conservative spirit of honoring the past over the present while being suspicious of secular designs for a perfect future. Dylan was a conservative because he was a radical in his critique of the modern world" (*ibid.*: 58). The words "radical" and "conservative" are used in a slippery way here, as they so often are in much writing about Dylan. But one of Webb's central claims is that Dylan's critique of, and despair at, the faults of the present was and is based on honouring rather than challenging tradition.

This view might sound plausible when thinking about Dylan's adoption and use of past musical styles, but it is misleading. Dylan has never been too worried about *conserving* or *preserving* the past as he has creatively appropriated it; he may have sought inspiration in the past, but he has transformed it as part of a critical engagement with living traditions. He has never been conserving music against future change. Webb's argument is misleading: honouring the past over the present is not necessarily informed by, nor does it inevitably lead to, conservative social or political beliefs, which is why artistic "revivals" (seeking value in the painting, poetry, architecture, music and drama of the past) have been both radical and conservative. It is also why country has been and can be both radical and conservative.

Dylan has drawn on country less for its apparent conservatism, and more for its stylistic appeal – the songs, the sounds and the lyrical imagery that he first heard during the 1950s. When he was growing up, he was impressed by the songs of Hank Williams and the expressive quality of his voice. Williams's music contains a direct form of vocal address and melodies drawn from hymns of the Southern churches, along with the mournful bent notes of the blues, and the imagery of railroads, bars and highways. There is an emotional, soulful vulnerability to his great songs of lost love and betrayal such as 'Lovesick Blues' or 'Cold, Cold, Heart' or 'I'm So Lonesome I Could Cry'. Dylan recorded Williams's 'Lonesome Whistle' during the *Freewheelin'* sessions and can be glimpsed performing 'Lost Highway' and a snatch of 'I'm So Lonesome I Could Cry' in the film *Don't Look Back*. Dylan recorded 'I Can't Get You Off My Mind' for a Hank Williams tribute album in 2001. Dylan (2004: 96) is not the only musician to have remarked on how songwriters can learn much about the poetics and structuring of songs by listening to Hank Williams.

Dylan was also very influenced by the Carter Family – A. P. Carter, his wife Sara and her cousin Maybellene, who first recorded in 1927 at the same Bristol, Tennessee, sessions as Jimmie Rodgers. Apart from their collection of songs, perhaps the most significant influence on Dylan is the guitar-playing technique developed by Maybellene (although Dylan was hardly alone in being influenced by this style). To give fullness and depth to their performances she created a style of guitar-playing that involved picking out a melodic lead line and strumming simultaneously – similar in aims, but quite distinct in sound, to what many solo blues musicians were doing. This guitar-playing style can be heard to great effect on one of their most well-known songs, 'Wildwood Flower' (available on various compilations). Dylan has used this guitar style throughout his performing career, on albums and in concert. It is noticeable on both *Freewheelin'* (1963) and *Good As I Been To You* (1993).

Dylan's admiration for the bluegrass style of the Stanley Brothers became apparent from the late 1990s, with the release of his recording of 'The Lonesome River' with Ralph Stanley on the album *Clinch Mountain Country*. It could also be heard in many shows around 1999–2001, which would include, and frequently start with, a Stanley Brothers song, notably 'Man Of Constant Sorrow', 'I Am The Man Thomas', 'Duncan And Brady', 'Hallelujah, I'm Ready To Go' and 'Somebody Touched Me'.

Dylan was friendly with Johnny Cash after meeting him in New York in 1963 and at the 1964 Newport Folk Festival. In 1969 they recorded many songs that didn't make it onto *Nashville Skyline* and around this time Cash began performing 'Wanted Man', a song the two musicians had written together. Dylan recorded 'Train Of Love' in 2002 as part of a tribute collection for the ill Johnny Cash. Dylan has also enjoyed a creative relationship with the prominent country maverick Willie Nelson. He worked with him on Farm Aid during the mid-1980s, and they jointly composed 'Heartland' in the early 1990s, a song that Dylan recorded with Nelson for the album *Across The Borderline* (1993). The two songwriters toured together during the summer of 2004.

There have been periods in Dylan's career as a musician when his debt to country music has been explicit, other times when it has been more disguised, as it was on *Blonde On Blonde*, considered by many to be one of Dylan's greatest albums and, with the exception of one track, recorded in Nashville. *Blonde On Blonde* is quite clearly influenced by country in the way Dylan adopts a relaxed and intimate vocal style, pitching his voice lower, singing closer to the microphone. *Blonde On Blonde* is pervaded by the staple themes of country – regret, remorse, melancholia, a certain resignation in the musical tones in contrast to the resilience or resistance of the blues. There is a vulnerability to his songs of longing and apology. The timbre of the vocals, the texture of the instruments, the ballad style, are all tinged with country hues; you can hear it most noticeably on 'Visions Of Johanna', 'One Of Us Must Know (Sooner Or Later)', 'Sad-Eyed Lady Of The Lowlands'. *Blonde On Blonde* gives intimations of the western folk ballad style of *John Wesley Harding* and the more "mainstream", warmer sound of

Nashville Skyline. All three albums feature the same producer, Bob Johnston, and two of the same musicians, Charlie McCoy and Kenny Buttrey.

Starting in 1994 with a rendition of the 1952 Pee Wee King hit 'You Belong To Me' for the soundtrack to *Natural Born Killers*, country has been the most significant thread in numerous Dylan recordings that have not featured on his albums. Apart from the tributes to Johnny Cash, Hank Williams and the Stanley Brothers during this time, further recordings include the countryish pop of 'Boogie Woogie Country Girl' on a tribute to Doc Pomus and 'Return To Me' for the *Sopranos* soundtrack; the more contemporary country of 'Ring Of Fire', a June Carter and Merle Kilgore song, for the film *Feeling Minnesota*; 'My Blue Eyed Jane' for a tribute to Jimmie Rodgers; the countryish rock'n'roll of 'Red Cadillac And A Black Moustache' on a Sun Records tribute; Dylan's own 'Waiting For You' for the soundtrack to the *Divine Secrets of the Ya-Ya Sisterhood*; his almost epic bluegrass ballad of 'Cross The Green Mountain' for the film *Gods and Generals*; his country shuffle 'Tell Ol' Bill' on the soundtrack to *North Country*. Dylan also included renditions of the traditional 'Diamond Joe' and 'Dixie' on the *Masked and Anonymous* soundtrack. An impressive country compilation could be put together from these recordings. The country feel has also been a feature of numerous live performances since 1999, when his bands have blended acoustic guitar with pedal steel, banjo or fiddle. It has been given a visual resonance by Dylan's appearance in stetson hat, bootlace tie, fringed shirts, piped trousers, embroidered jackets or frockcoats (the apparel that has come to be associated with country performers).

Folk

When Dylan first began to receive critical acclaim during the early 1960s he was recognized and understood as a folk singer. Yet it is impossible to make any fine distinction between blues, country and folk music. Blues and country spring from folk sources, often using the same musical and lyrical patterns, and sharing the folk approach to composition. As Pete Seeger once put it when asked to characterize folk music,

> "First of all it's a process. It's not any particular song, it's not any particular singer. It's a process by which ordinary people take over old songs and make them their own. They don't just

> listen to it. They sing it. They sing along with it. And they
> change it." (Zollo 2003: 5)

Folk is a living engagement with existing songs as much as it might be about any recognizable style or tradition. This is why many popular musicians have felt the inclination to say something along the lines that "all music is folk music".

When Dylan was playing rock'n'roll in the mid-1950s, folk songs had been acquiring value among educated city-dwellers and intellectuals, those who were seeking something more authentic than what was circulated by the media and music business. The folk song "revival" of the 1950s was but the latest of a series of revivals that had occurred regularly since the late eighteenth century. There was a notable wave of interest in folk song in the late nineteenth century, across Europe and the United States, when middle-class song collectors (and many composers) valued the apparent timeless-ness, common sense and ancient characteristics of folk custom and set out to preserve and make use of it. In the twentieth century a further revival of interest in folk music was provoked by anxiety about new forms of "mass culture" – recorded sound, radio, film and television. From the 1930s, many intellectuals feared that the public was becoming an amorphous "mass" of uncritical consumers, losing touch with the roots of their own culture, duped and manipulated by advertising, marketing and public relations.

The interest in folk during the late nineteenth and early twentieth centuries had been conservative, a longing for a golden age, before people were corrupted by cities, industries, mass media and commerce. In contrast, the renewed interest in folk that grew during the 1950s was informed by a more radical, often explicitly socialist or communist, agenda that stressed the way ordinary people had to struggle to make their own art and to find a voice. This provoked an interest in folk songs associated with or depicting cities, industry and working life. Folk music was no longer about a search for a bygone rural idyll. It was grittier, earthier – it was real. Folk singers sang about the plight of working men and women, they sang about romance, infidelity, sex, drinking, violence, crime, politics and war. This was the context within which Dylan became a folk singer.

The 1950s folk revival was fed by compilation albums that displayed a rich and varied musical history, which often ran counter to, rather than being supportive of, official definitions of the United States as a unified nation. In the folk circles of Greenwich Village the *Anthology of American Folk Music* was profoundly influential and had a lasting impact on Dylan. This was a selection of recordings that had been initially released between 1927 and 1932, and came from a record collection accumulated by the bohemian maverick Harry Smith. It was compiled in collaboration with Moe Asch and released in 1952 by Folkways Records, as six LP records containing 84 tracks. For many listeners it was as if a sonic archaeologist had excavated and discovered a hidden, previously inaudible, musical world. Although it didn't sell a lot of copies, it had a huge influence in folk circles. For many musicians it was the first time they had heard Blind Willie Johnson, Mississippi John Hurt and Blind Lemon Jefferson. Dave Van Ronk, a contemporary of Dylan's, remembers it as providing "a classical education that we all shared in common, whatever our personal differences" (2006: 47). People passed it round or listened collectively, and it has continued to inspire new generations of musicians whenever it has been reissued. The *Anthology* ranges through ballads, spirituals and hymns, and dance tunes, constantly shifting from the light and frivolous to the profound and sometimes macabre. Smith presented it with minimal notes about each song and did not categorize artists by their race. Many of the recordings seemed to conjure up "an old weird America" (Marcus 1997), a more radical, diverse and freer idea of the nation, and appealed to those on the left. Greil Marcus has written of how Smith

> ignored all field recordings, Library of Congress archives, anything validated only by scholarship or carrying the must of the museum. He wanted music to which people had really responded: records put on sale that at least somebody thought were worth paying for. (*ibid*.: 102)

Marcus points to an ideological division between those who valued an idyllic music of the people, seemingly untouched by commerce, and those who recognized that a repertoire of folk songs existed on discs issued by record companies. Although there were clear overlaps between these two constituencies, when Dylan embraced folk music during 1959–60 he entered a scene populated by people who had rigid ideas about what folk music was, where it had come from, how it should be played and who should play it. Compared to the rock'n'roll he had been performing in Hibbing a few years earlier, this was music with a long history, approached from a variety of musical and political perspectives, collected, written about and debated by people who set themselves up as authorities. Dylan would very soon become aware of what he has called the "folk police" (2004: 248) and distance himself from the idea that a folk singer could represent anyone ("the people", "the negro race", "the proletariat") but him or herself.

The influence of folk music can be heard immediately in Dylan's voice. Like blues singers, folk performers flatten and bend notes and use intervals and intonation that are far removed from the classical approach to pitch and scales. Being for many years a mainly unaccompanied form – songs delivered by single or collective voices – there was never any "functional" need for folk melodies to connect with an underlying harmony (which is why classically trained musicians had great difficulty when they tried to add chords and particularly when trying to arrange folk songs for the piano).

For a brief period Dylan imitated Woody Guthrie's manner of delivering a narrative in a semi-spoken talking blues, along with his rural Okie accent and approach to songwriting. Dylan's engagement with Guthrie's music and performing style contributed to the development of his own distinct sound and he soon moved away from obvious mimicry. Guthrie's voice is warmer, less harsh than Dylan's, and not as nasal, not as bluesy. The enduring influence of Woody Guthrie on Bob Dylan can be heard less in Dylan's voice or songwriting and more in his attitude and approach to the way that a song is performed. Dylan had owned a copy of Guthrie's songbook *California to the New York Island*, a book in which he had written "the property of Bob Dylan". As Clinton Heylin recounts in his biography, Dylan had also highlighted a section in Pete Seeger's introduction to the book, as follows:

> Beware of trying to imitate Woody's singing too closely – it will sound fake and phoney.
> 1. Don't try and imitate his accent.
> 2. Don't try and imitate his flat vocal quality.
> 3. In short, be yourself.
> What any singer can learn from Woody's method of performance are such things as this:
> 1. A matter-of-fact, unmelodramatic, understatement throughout.
> 2. Simplicity above all – and getting the words out clearly. They are the most important part of the song.

3. Irregularity.
This last perhaps needs explanation: to avoid a sing-song effect, from repeating the same simple melody many times, Woody, like all American ballad singers, held out long notes in unexpected places, although his guitar strumming maintained an even tempo. Thus no two verses sounded alike. Extra beats were often added to measures. (Heylin 2000: 82)

Simplicity, understatement, irregularity and adopting an approach to phrasing that uses notes in unexpected places are musical characteristics of the folk aesthetic, features that link folk and blues and which underpin an approach to performance as transformative, challenging a distinction between composing a new song and giving a rendition of an existing song. Songs are explored during performance and this becomes a means of developing them, making them fit new circumstances.

Right at the beginning of Dylan's career as a successful songwriter he appropriated, absorbed and recast 'No More Auction Block', a tune from the folk spiritual tradition and used it as a basis for 'Blowin' In The Wind'. He had been particularly influenced by Odetta's version of this song, Odetta being a performer who had a significant formative impact on Dylan. As he recalled:

"The first thing that turned me on to folk singing was Odetta. I heard a record of hers in a record store, back when you could listen to records right there in the store ... I went out and traded my electric guitar and amplifier for an acoustical guitar, a flat-top Gibson." (Rosenbaum 1978: 64)

Folk, blues and acoustic gospel blurred in Odetta's performances, and Dylan was influenced by the forceful way that the rhythms of her strummed guitar interacted with the vocal delivery of lyrics. Dylan began performing other Odetta arrangements, such as 'Jack Of Diamonds', but it was 'No More Auction Block' (sometimes known as 'Many Thousands Gone') that was to be particularly important in the life of Bob Dylan.

According to Oliver Trager, the lyrics (beginning "No more auction block for me") were first sung by slaves who escaped to Canada after Britain abolished slavery in 1833 (in the USA slavery was not completely abolished until 1865). It was later published in printed form by the *Atlantic Monthly* in 1867 and evidence suggests that it may have been sung by marching ex-slaves who had joined the Union forces after escaping the Confederate army. The melody is thought to be traceable to the Ashanti tribe of West Africa (Trager 2004).

The only recording of Dylan performing this song was made at the Gaslight Café in October 1962 (available on *The Bootleg Series Volume 1*), with him tentatively picking out the melody on acoustic guitar. This performance was described by John Bauldie as "a young white boy somehow conjuring the persona of the singer, the exhausted, the newly liberated slave acknowledging his deliverance" (1991: 6) and by Paul Williams as a voice that combines both strength and vulnerability, "He sings ... not with the fire of one who's been there but with great dignity, as if he wants to acknowledge the power of what he's felt and learned ... from songs like this one" (1990: 67).

The melody became the basis for one of Dylan's best-known songs, a source that many in Greenwich Village immediately spotted and one that Dylan openly acknowledged in a radio interview in 1978:

> "'Blowin' In The Wind' has always been a spiritual. I took it off a song called 'No More Auction Block' – that's a spiritual and 'Blowin' In The Wind' sorta follows the same feeling ... I just did it on my acoustic guitar when I recorded it, which didn't really make it sound spiritual. But the feeling, the idea, was always, you know, that's where it was coming from, so now I'm doing it in full like a spiritual." (Rowland 1978)

In concerts around this time, Dylan began emphasizing the spiritual qualities by allowing the female vocalists to become more prominent.

During the summer of 1981 the stage version of 'Blowin' In The Wind' began with backing vocalists singing the first verse, accompanied only by sparse revivalist-style organ, before being joined by full-bodied gospel-style church organ, and then a somewhat foreboding, ominous rhythm doubled up on bass and drums, with the band almost beating out a slow march, a ghostly echo of tramping footsteps of freed slaves. The older song lived on inside Dylan's new composition, but we can't really treat either as "original" in the way that the term is often used, more as contributions to a living tradition.

The exploration of an existing song becomes the basis for the development of another song and this folk philosophy is central to Dylan's songwriting. So, for example, 'A Hard Rain's A-Gonna Fall' takes its starting-point from an old ballad, 'Lord Randall', whose opening lines are "Oh where ha' you been, Lord Randall, my son? And where ha' you been, my handsome young man?" 'Girl From The North Country' appropriates and transforms the melody and lyrics of 'Scarborough Fair'. There are many more examples from this early acoustic period, including 'Masters Of War', which draws on the tune of 'Fair Nottamun Town', 'With God On Our Side', which uses the tune of 'The Patriot Game', and 'Bob Dylan's Dream', which draws on 'Lady Franklin's Lament'. 'Don't Think Twice, It's All Right' uses the melody from a song Paul Clayton had recorded and copyrighted as 'Who's Goin' To Buy You Ribbons When I'm Gone?', which in turn drew on older traditional songs with the titles 'Who's Gonna Buy Your Chickens [Flowers] When I'm Gone?' Johnny Cash used the same melody for his song 'Understand Your Man'.

When Dylan began 'It Ain't Me, Babe' by singing "Go away from my window" he was drawing on various nineteenth-century songs that began "Oh, get away from the window", a phrase that goes back, at least, to a song in the Jacobean play *The Knight of the Burning Pestle*, the opening line of which was written down in 1613 as "Go from my window, love, goe" (Van der Merwe 1989: 70). When Dylan composed 'Ballad In Plain D' he used the melody of an old folk tune that can be found in songs such as 'Once I Had A Sweetheart' and 'The False Bride'.

In Dylan's subsequent songs the melodic and lyrical connections are sometimes not so obvious, and judgements may vary from listener to listener. Similarities have been spotted between 'Maggie's Farm' and Pete Seeger's 'Penny's Farm'; 'Obviously Five Believers' and 'Me And My Chauffeur Blues' by Memphis Minnie, and also Bo Diddley's 'She's Fine, She's Mine'; 'Leopard-Skin Pill-Box Hat' is said to resemble Lightning Hopkins's 'Automobile Blues' (although both would seem to be siblings in a huge family of similar blues). 'I Pity The Poor Immigrant' is adapted from the melody of a traditional Scottish ballad 'Come All Ye Tramps And Hawkers'. 'If You See Her, Say Hello' is said to be derived from 'Tell Him I Said Hello' by Bill Hagner and Jack Canning. 'Blind Willie McTell' draws on McTell's 'The Dyin' Crapshooter's Blues', which in turn draws on an old British ballad 'The Unfortunate Rake', which also feeds into 'St. James Infirmary Blues', famously recorded by Louis Armstrong and rather dubiously credited to Joe Primrose, a pseudonym of the music publisher Irving Mills. Dylan drops an oblique acknowledgement of this connection by referring in the lyrics to looking out of the window of the "St James Hotel".

When Dylan released "Love And Theft" in 2001, fans and detractors alike were excited by the way it self-consciously, and occasionally ironically, acknowledged that the songs had been sourced via an activity signalled in the title – "love and theft". The internet now enabled aficionados and journalists to swap references they had discovered. Whereas Dylan's sources in the early 1960s had been traditional folk ballads and blues, he was now drawing extensively from commercial pop songs. Well-supported claims were put forward for striking musical similarities between 'Tweedle Dee & Tweedle Dum' and 'Uncle John's Bongos' by Johnnie and Jack (1961); 'Bye And Bye' and Billie Holiday's performance of 'Having Myself A Time' by Leo Robin and Ralph Rainger (1938); 'Floater' and 'Snuggled On Your Shoulders' by Carmen Lombardo and Joe Young (1932); 'Sugar Baby' and 'The Lonesome Road' by Gene Austin and Nathaniel Shilkret (1928). It continued on *Modern Times*: 'Thunder On The Mountain' quite clearly resembles the melody of Chuck Berry's 'Johnny B. Goode' (1958); 'When The Deal Goes Down' uses some of the melodies of 'Where The Blue Of The Night Meets The Gold Of The Day' by Roy Turk and Fred Ahlert, famously performed by Bing Crosby (1931); 'Rollin' And Tumblin'' (a stock blues phrase anyway) recycles Muddy Waters's performance of 'Roll And Tumble Blues' (1950), the earliest recording of which seems to have been by Hambone Willie Newbern in 1929; 'Beyond The Horizon' is based on Jimmy Kennedy's 'Red Sails In The Sunset' (1935); 'The Levee's Gonna Break' draws heavily from 'When The Levee Breaks', recorded in 1929 by Kansas Joe McCoy and Memphis Minnie; and 'Someday Baby' draws on a whole family of songs that pass through various versions of 'Worried Life Blues'. In all cases Dylan signals his debt musically by using some of the same melodies, chords, solos and arrangements.

Dylan has quite clearly been having fun with these two albums. After forty years of having people obsessively sift through his songs (not to mention his personal possessions and garbage) for clues about his personality, family life, political views and religious beliefs, he was now putting it all together from existing words and tunes, and seeming to undermine the idea that these songs were the expression of a unique musician. The more you look at the lyrics and listen to the tunes, the more "Bob Dylan" disappears. In many ways it is the ultimate undisguised consequence of what he's been doing ever since he started songwriting. As he has said of the way he writes songs,

> "What happens is, I'll take a song I know and simply start playing it in my head. That's the way I meditate. A lot of people will look at a crack on the wall and meditate, or count sheep or angels or money or something, and it's a proven fact that it'll help them relax. I don't meditate on any of that stuff. I meditate on a song. I'll be playing Bob Nolan's 'Tumbling Tumbleweeds', for instance, in my head constantly – while I'm driving a car or talking to a person or sitting around or whatever. People will think they are talking to me and I'm talking back, but I'm not. I'm listening to the song in my head. At a certain point, some of the words will change and I'll start writing a song." (Hilburn 2005: 74)

The issue for the folk guardians in the early 1960s and the plagiarism police forty years later concerns whether Dylan should formally acknowledge his sources: is it the folk process or stealing? In his biography Shelton remembered:

> By the end of 1963, the folk scene was bitterly divided over whether Dylan was a song cribber or a composer working in the accepted tradition of building on skeletal remains. By the late autumn of 1963, when a claim was made on the melody of 'Don't Think Twice', even Grossman [Dylan's manager] began to worry. I suggested to Grossman that Dylan indicate on his albums and in his folios some of the songs' folk sources. I hinted that there must be instances where Dylan wasn't certain where he got a phrase or melodic idea. "He knows, all right," Grossman replied dryly. (1986: 163)

Shelton then quotes the ethnomusicologist Charles Seeger (father of Pete, Peggy and Mike) saying that artistic creation is characterized by "conscious and unconscious appropriation, borrowing, adapting, plagiarizing and plain stealing" and that "the folk song is, by definition, and, as far as we can tell, by reality, entirely a product of plagiarism" (*ibid.*: 164).

Accusations of stealing have followed Dylan since he started. A particularly droll intervention occurred during a press conference in 1965 when Allen Ginsberg asked, "Do you ever think there will ever be a time when you'll be hung as a thief?" (Gray 2006: 256). For some internet bloggers that time had arrived with the blatant copying of melodies, arrangements and solos on *"Love And Theft"* and *Modern Times*.

In an age when the music industry and media are obsessed with intellectual property, Dylan's songwriting is considered by many to involve a provocative creative strategy. It raises acute questions that go to the heart of what it means to create music as part of a living vernacular tradition.

Yet, music listeners are rarely worried by such issues. Many of the pleasures that come from popular music listening – for non-playing audience members and fellow musicians alike – arise from those moments of sudden recognition or discovery, when we find a connection between one song and another, when we detect a deliberate or coincidental link in a chain back to previous songs, music and traditions. This happens constantly in all popular music genres. There is a vast archive of songs and music (ever more accessible through the digitalization of catalogues), a huge web of connections across and within genres that provides endless opportunities for sonic adventures and musical voyages of discovery. Many people have been introduced to an entire history of folk and blues through Dylan's songs. Dylan is by no means alone in having fans who obsessively spend hours of fun sifting through his tunes and lyrics, finding connections to other songs, tracing various sources and influences. The similarities between songs do not undermine their value for the audience. It is part of the experience.

At the same time, all the moralizing about copying detracts from the imaginative and highly idiosyncratic way that Dylan has consciously taken or unconsciously absorbed both lyrics and tunes. Many of Dylan's melodies and lyrics are drawn from folk and blues idioms in which numerous songs share similar melodies and lyrics. Yet many are derived from more mainstream styles of popular music, the creation of which involves the same type of chain of influence and use. Explicitly copying, appropriating and transforming existing songs and music is fundamental to the creativity of popular music. It is not unusual. It is the norm.

Every great pop songwriter has drawn melodic inspiration from elsewhere. Sometimes it has been quite deliberate, as in John Lennon's use of the melody, riff and bits of lyric from Chuck Berry's 'You Can't Catch Me' in 'Come Together' (a case that was settled out of court). Sometimes it has been unintentional, as when George Harrison inadvertently reused the melody and chords of 'He's So Fine' by the Chiffons in 'My Sweet Lord' (and was forced to settle via the court). Theories of individual ownership, laws of copyright and the notion of identifiable intellectual property are quite contrary to the way music has been made in numerous folk traditions that feed into contemporary popular music.

4 Lyrics

Bob Dylan began writing songs at a time when the boundaries between folk, commercial pop and high art were being questioned. Dylan's lyrics constantly challenged these categories, often to the annoyance of the guardians of genres. Traditional folk singers hated the way he embraced the sounds and styles of pop, rock'n'roll and electric blues; pop fans were suspicious of how the three-minute frivolous song had lost its innocence, acquiring unnecessary intelligence and artistic pretension; the high-art establishment was sceptical of claims being made for a new poetry that was bridging the old barriers between low and high culture. Dylan drew inspiration for his lyrics from such apparently diverse sources as Robert Johnson, Arthur Rimbaud, Hank Williams, T. S. Eliot, beat poetry, the Bible, 1950s pop, Chuck Berry, Hollywood movies and five-hundred-year-old ballads.

Dylan's lyrics questioned the idea that there were separate audiences for pop, folk and art, and exposed the arbitrary character of such categories. He influenced his contemporaries and future generations of songwriters, and altered the expectations of listeners. He brought to pop music the rugged earthiness of the folk ballad and blues holler, but linked them to a more introverted literary sensibility. The three- or four-minute commercial song now had the potential to depict and dramatize the more tortuous and troubling side of sex and romance; it could use symbolism to convey ideas and sensations for which ordinary words and phrases seemed inadequate. Songs could comment on society, politics and prejudice, singers could "protest" and perhaps play some part in the struggle to bring about a better world.

As Dylan's recordings circulated beyond the folk crowd, many who began arguing about the meaning of his songs were university-educated, often with a background in the liberal arts. Yet music fans with little knowledge of poetry and literature were also drawn to his words. It is hard now to imagine the first impact of seeing Dylan out on stage alone, listening to the sparse, rhythmic acoustic guitar accompaniment and vulnerable harmonica, as he performed songs such as 'It's Alright, Ma (I'm Only Bleeding)', with fifteen verses and five varying choruses; or 'Desolation Row', with its ten long verses, each concluding with the title phrase; or the blend of mystical and mundane metaphors that pervade 'Visions Of Johanna' and 'Mr. Tambourine Man'. Songs were stretched out in performance, lasting well over ten minutes. Audiences sat attentively, quietly, trying to catch all the words, not out of politeness or respect. Many who attended remember being stunned, spellbound and amazed by the sheer number of rhymes, images, ideas and associations conjured up, as well as the evocative intensity of Dylan's expressive voice and mournful harmonica.

As rock music became a distinct category, from about 1964 to 1966, the writings of literary critics connected with an educated, mildly bohemian, middle-class audience eager to elevate popular songs as a new poetic art. A space appeared in the alternative or "underground" press where Dylan's lyrics were dissected for their political relevance and aesthetic value.

Over the years, literary scholars have spent hours poring over Dylan's lyrics, attempting to detect his sources, to identify his influences and to track various cross-references, analysing the combination of words, patterns of rhyme, and metre of verses. The songs have been grouped into categories according to recurring themes, and critics have produced a plethora of often highly speculative, occasionally ridiculous, interpretations of various phrases, lines, verses and entire songs.

Dylan's lyrics have been used and abused, appropriated and interpreted, enlisted and twisted by numerous people – read as art, as politics, as autobiography and as a sign of the times. It has been assumed that Dylan's song lyrics can tell us a lot about their author, his listeners and their society. At the same time, they have looked to the lyrics for intimations of a more transcendent or universal artistic and moral truth. Dylan's words have been forced to meet many expectations and his lyrics have been burdened with much baggage.

Literary criticism: professors, philosophers and fans

Dylan's songs have been treated as poetry on a page, worthy of exegesis by the techniques of high art criticism. Christopher Ricks has pursued this course, combining the assurance of a well-read professor of English Literature and the understandings of a passionate Dylan fan. He is an imaginative, skilful writer who peppers his prose with all manner of clever allusions, in-jokes and puns when making arguments such as this:

> Satire, yes, these Skeltonic raids and forays, but the song is not ready for to fade into its own tirade. It has the wisdom to mock not only the complacencies of Polonius but the inverted (cynical) complacencies of Hamlet, who first mocks and then kills Polonius. (Ricks 2003: 257)

This is an extract from a celebration of the lyrics of 'Subterranean Homesick Blues'. I'm not sure it is the same song that I know, but Ricks can journey to unexpected places and attempts to convince the reader of the value of his routes through the pyrotechnics of his prose and the unusual associations this conjures up. Of the Dylan song 'Not Dark Yet' he rhetorically puns "*Not Dark Yet* is owed to a nightingale" (*ibid.*: 361), encouraging us to notice similarities between Keats's poem ("Ode to a Nightingale") and Dylan's song. He then makes a move that seems to be obligatory in the lit. crit. approach to Dylan – he takes us back to Shakespeare:

> *Not Dark Yet* stands to Keats's *Ode* very much as Keats's *Ode*, in turn, stood to Shakespeare's Sonnet 73, "That time of year thou mayst in me behold". The continuity and community of poets constitute a success that is a succession. (*ibid.*: 367)

Michael Gray writes as an independent scholar and journalist, close to Ricks in his concern with poetry, and explicit about valuing Dylan's lyrics as a challenge to "the lit mob's traditional hostility to the idea of Bob Dylan as among the worthy" (2000: 249). Gray's strategy entails blending insights from painstaking research into the sources of Dylan's lyrics (in rhymes, ballads, blues, poetry and literature) with appreciative but also quite scathing commentaries on their literary merit. Although frequently perceptive, he can be quite disdainful, often adopting the tone of a miserable schoolteacher with an overactive red pen, particularly when complaining about the "sloppiness" of some of Dylan's lyrical constructions: "Come on, Bob. If *you* were your English teacher you'd put your red pencil through this. Could do better" (*ibid.*: 465) – that about 'License To Kill'. Gray is continually agitated about syntax and constantly castigates Dylan for his grammar. Of 'Emotionally Yours' he writes of the "failure" of one of Dylan's "conspicuous rhymes" because "a verb our ears are accustomed to hearing as transitive is used as an intransitive one, and sounds awkward in consequence" (*ibid.*: 569), and of 'Dark Eyes' he complains because Dylan uses the phrase "'to slide' ... without a preposition after it" (*ibid.*), which apparently "sounds awkward". These, and many other similar criticisms, are the result of reading the lyrics as poetry on a page, and seemingly forgetting that they are words in a pop song. They are sung, used to convey sentiment, gesture and expression. It is not a grammatical exercise in communication. I find it just as pointless when critics concur with Dave Van Ronk's argument that the lyric to 'All Along The Watchtower' is flawed and "sloppy" because "a watchtower is not a road or a wall, and you can't go along it" (2006: 208). Well, you can go along it in a song. You can do lots of odd things in songs.

A more academic approach is adopted by Aidan Day (1988), who is explicitly concerned with "reading the lyrics of Bob Dylan" (the subtitle of his book). Day is interested in how Dylan's songs address more profound and abstract philosophical questions about identity. Although a specialist in English literature, he does not seek grammatical correctness nor engage in flights of linguistic fancy, but searches for a deeper truth in Dylan's lyrics. Here are just some of his reflections on the final verses of 'Desolation Row':

> The speaker in the last stanza insists on an inability to read the received narratives and asserts that only rewritten versions – versions scripted, like those of this lyric, from desolation's perspective – are acceptable. But the desolating double-bind explored by this lyric is that the rearrangement – the felt necessity to rewrite – can itself stand as a manifestation of the ill pervading the culture rather than a revolutionary act which transcends that ill. The act of fracturing and redistributing – disturbing the surface patterns of approved culture – is indistinguishable in the lyric from the inherent disorder which the act of disturbance sets out to expose. "These fragments I have shored against my ruins" observes a voice towards the end of T. S. Eliot's *The Waste*

> *Land.* The poetic practices of 'Desolation Row' owe a debt to
> the work of such as T. S. Eliot. Yet even as the lyric pursues
> that inheritance it is conscious too of the possible fruitless-
> ness of assuming that ruin may be fought with or healed by
> ruin. (1988: 89)

Like Ricks, Day connects Dylan's lyrics to the high literary tradition, but he
is more interested in the philosophy than the poetics. This is typical of a
certain tendency in writings about Dylan. As Gray has pointed out, Day treats
Dylan's song lyrics as if they were "a philosophy essay". Songs are
approached as if they express a coherent system of thought, and inevitably
Day ends up with lots of philosophical conundrums that he can't answer. A
discussion of the lyrics to 'Jokerman' is punctuated with questions such as:

> In 'Jokerman', are the Christological stature of the figure that
> stands on the water and walks on the clouds, and the mystical
> exaltation of the man of the mountains, evidences of an
> authentic and authenticated spiritual capacity, evidences of
> access to some form of verifiable higher authority? (1988: 140)

A few lines later, contemplating the Jokerman's apparently uncaring qualities,
he asks, "Is it a carelessness transfigured by its attention to an absolute that
providentially guarantees the world's rescue?" (*ibid.*: 141). The unanswerable
or rhetorical questions flow and we seem to lose all sight of the fact that
Dylan is, actually, a musician and songwriter.

A more self-consciously "common-sense" and pragmatic approach to
Dylan's lyrics can be found in the writings of Andrew Muir, a writer who
starts by singling out Day's book as one that few people he knows have
managed to read all the way through. Muir is a fan who has edited a number
of Dylan magazines and calls his approach "analytical but understandable"
(2003: vii). Although "using the tools of literary criticism", he is careful not
to forget that he is "discussing song lyrics rather than poems and that they
have to be heard not read" (*ibid.*: x). Unlike overtly theoretical approaches
to the subject, he stresses his subjective experience:

> I am telling you how the songs make me think and feel and
> why and how I think they come to do so. I hope by doing this

that I in some way deepen your understanding of and/or
appreciation of Dylan's songs. (*ibid.*: xiv)

Muir is one of the more insightful of the critical fans who write for the Dylan
magazines. He has provided a vivid, fan's-eye view of Dylan's touring during
the 1990s (Muir 2001) and produced a number of carefully researched
articles that demonstrate in detail Dylan's debt to folk ballads (Muir 2003).
As a fan he is more concerned with the sincerity of Dylan's songs than their
formal qualities. Of 'To Make You Feel My Love', Muir writes:

> It beggars belief that the man who has just sung so expres-
> sively on 'Tryin' To Get To Heaven' does not realize how
> insincere this sounds. Without wishing to sound too ageist
> about it – wasn't Dylan a bit old to be coming across like a
> lovesick teenager? Whatever the answer to that, he com-
> pletely lacks conviction here. Everything negative about the
> album is represented on this one track; sloppy writing, hor-
> rendous sound, insincere bluffing of the audience. Compare
> and contrast the way he sings "lurve" here and the "a-beatin"
> in the previous songs. (2003: 235)

Any type of music criticism is judgemental, by the nature of the exercise.
Here Muir's sense of authority, his moral superiority in writing such criticism,
resides in the fan's desire for sincerity – in contrast to the imaginative
poetics that fascinate Ricks or the incorrect grammar that vexes Gray, or the
philosophical conundrums that entice Day. Muir is attuned to the words as
performance and picks up on the way words are sung as crucial to the
meaning of the song. Yet he brings to his interpretation a tone of moral
censure because the song's sentiments do not equate with his understanding
of the correct behaviour for people of Dylan's age. Don't older people fall
in love? Has Dylan passed some age limit when he's no longer allowed to
sing about romance? With the rhetorical phrase "compare and contrast",
Muir reduces commentary to the logic of a school exam paper or classroom
exercise. When he writes about 'Tryin' To Get To Heaven', Muir even
acknowledges that Dylan has said "it's definitely a performance record instead of a poetic literary type of thing". He then still has the confidence to
write, "No Dylan listener I know would mind that at all. It does not,

however, excuse poor lyrics; there is a recognisable difference between good, simple lyrics and sloppy, poor lyrics that are simple in the pejorative sense" (*ibid.*: 231).

Muir's moralizing censure is far removed from Ricks's celebratory flights of the imagination. Ricks allows us to observe Dylan as a member of a pantheon of poets; Day asks us a series of profound questions about Dylan's philosophy; Gray encourages us to pass judgement on the more pragmatic way Dylan uses language; as does Muir, who also alerts us to the fan's constant, if naïve, concern with the distant musician's sincerity and the authenticity of sentiments in his songs. None of this literary criticism is too bothered about the power, persuasiveness and *musicality* of the lyrics, although Ricks is acutely attuned to the rhythms, timing and sounds of the words as both ordinary speech and extraordinary poetry. An alternative to literary criticism is to hear the words as autobiography.

Song and self

In his largely literary study, Stephen Scobie confesses: "Many Bob Dylan fans, myself included, have an almost obsessive (or 'bobsessive') interest in the details of his biography" (2003: 84). Scobie is wary of linking biographical details to Dylan's lyrics, particularly those addressing love and relationships, and argues that they should be approached as dramatic images rather than as clues in a biographical "crossword puzzle" (*ibid.*: 87). Scobie just about manages to follow this principle in his book, but other writers have no qualms about judging the lyrics according to what is known of Dylan's life story, as in the following comments made by Clinton Heylin about the songs on *Blood On The Tracks*:

> And yet an air of self-delusion blows through many of the songs. On 'Idiot Wind' and 'If You See Her, Say Hello,' the male narrator paints himself as the wronged party while the central male figures in 'Tangled Up In Blue' and 'Lily, Rosemary And The Jack Of Hearts' take on quite heroic proportions … In real life, though, it was Dylan who had been unfaithful and, far from behaving heroically, he had simply kept running from responsibility… (2000: 385)

Here the lyrics are enlisted for a moral judgement about the lack of conso-
nance between Dylan's "real life" and his songs. Quite apart from the
reliability of any information and gossip that leads Heylin to such an argument, why should the lyrics of a popular song correspond to real events, and
then be morally evaluated as a distortion or conceit on the part of the
songwriter? The songs that Heylin mentions are not the most obvious personal communiqués from real life. He cites 'Idiot Wind' – a lyric that starts
with a first-person narrator who's been accused of shooting "a man named
Gray" and taking his wife to Italy. He mentions 'Tangled Up In Blue' – a song
that appears to have multiple narrators, protagonists and perspectives. He
refers to 'Lily, Rosemary And The Jack Of Hearts' – a long, rambling 16-verse
narrative that sounds like a country and western tale from the Wild West
world of escapist 1950s B-movies. As for the "heroic proportions" of the
central male characters, folk ballads, like films and novels are meant to
contain heroes – no matter how unheroic the director, author or composer.
Why assume that the dramatic imagery must be a reflection or provide clues
to events in Dylan's "real life"?

Songs seem to encourage the biographical and "real-life" approach, in part
because they are usually written in a direct way with the first person "I" often
addressing a "you". Great pop songwriters have always been aware of the
ambiguities of "I" and "you" and of the different ways that audiences will
identify with a song (how the "I" or "you" can stand in for me, her, him).
Yet many listeners hear the "I" as always the singer rather than a character
or narrator, and assume the lyric refers to a real rather than an imaginary
event. The song 'She's Your Lover Now' prompted Paul Williams to embark
on rambling speculations about this and other songs of the mid-1960s with
these thoughts: "I have no idea what biographical event could have inspired
this song – this is a guy who just got married in November, whose first child
is about to be born, maybe he's harking back to an earlier incident – who
knows?" (1990: 179-80).

Also seeking biographical motives for songs, Gray wished to impose a
very particular interpretation on *Under The Red Sky*:

> It is unsurprising that in middle age, and with his own children
> grown, Bob Dylan should revisit the arena of the nursery
> rhyme and the fairy tale. Like me, he is the sort of age at
> which re-examinations of the central self, impelled by what is

not called the "mid-life" crisis for nothing, become unavoidable and important. (2000: 666)

Here the motive for Dylan's songwriting is reduced to a one-dimensional life
trajectory, a claim supported by an apparent correspondence between the
experience of the critic and the life of the musician ("like me ..."). Although
Gray was undoubtedly not aware of it, at the time Dylan had a four-year-old
daughter with his second wife Carolyn. This implies an alternative explanation:
the album is less a morbidly nostalgic response to middle-age angst that
Dylan shares with Gray and more a joyful celebration of the pleasure of
singing nursery-type rhymes and making up new fairy tales for a young child.
That is Paul Williams's interpretation:

> It sounds ... like an album made by a songwriter who's spend-
> ing a lot of time this winter with his two very young children
> ... Listen to Dylan's *performance* of 'Wiggle Wiggle' and of
> the album's second song ['Under The Red Sky'] ... and you can
> hear clearly how much he loves his small children and there-
> fore life itself, his life right now ... (2004: 260–1)

These are two quite contrasting biographical explanations and say more about
the listener than the song, let alone the songwriter. The irony, of course,
is that I have stepped into the same circle by using biographical information
to challenge arguments based on biographical information.

There are certainly a few Dylan songs where the lyrics have an unambiguous relationship to identifiable events in his life, as he has acknowledged. For
example, 'Day Of The Locusts' impressionistically evokes Dylan's bewilder-
ment, detachment and desire to flee on the occasion when he was awarded
an honorary degree at Princeton. 'Ballad In Plain D' is an account of the
break-up of his relationship with Suze Rotolo and the tensions with her sister
Carla. Of this song Dylan later remarked, "I don't write confessional songs
... well, actually I did write one once and it wasn't very good – it was a
mistake to record and I regret it" (Crowe 1985: 51–2). Of this song he also
recalled:

> "That one I look back at and say, 'I must have been a real
> schmuck to write that.' I look back at that particular one and

say, of all the songs I've written, maybe that one could have been left alone … At that time my audience was very small. It overtook my mind so I wrote it. Maybe I shouldn't have used that. I had other songs at the time. It was based on an old folk song." (Flanagan 1987: 97)

Many of the songs on *Blood On The Tracks* are intense ruminations and reflections on love, loss and relationships. The album was recorded during a time in the mid-1970s when it was public knowledge that Dylan was separated from his wife Sara, which is why this album has prompted biographical interpretations. It is surely misleading to treat the songs on *Blood On The Tracks* as a straightforward autobiographical account of Dylan's life and relationships. It would be equally naïve to suppose that the album can be treated as self-contained fiction and imaginative invention, quite independent from the songwriter's experiences. A dynamic tension connects creative work to personal experience. Even the most rational and methodical of actors and actresses can find that their on-screen or stage role is creeping into their "personal" life or that their "private" identity manifests itself in unexpected ways in their fictional performance. As Dave Laing has remarked, "There can be no absolute boundary between autobiography's rhetoric of 'truth' and fiction's rhetoric of 'artifice'" (2005: 269). This is what makes human identities, art, music and performance so fascinating.

This tension is inescapable when we listen to songs, and it can lead to all manner of apparent paradoxes. Songs are "fictions" that are sung by "characters" using the codes and conventions of genres and "performed" on stages. Songs are sung by real people, using everyday language, and are drawn from their experience of life. It is naïve to assume that there is a direct relationship between the human being singing and the sentiments of the song, any more than there is a straightforward connection between a novel and its author, or an actress and a role. Yet it is surely denying our practical experience of human dialogue to assume that the singers, writers and actors tell us nothing about themselves and only about the characters they inhabit (or the Bob Dylan mask). Songs can tell us a lot about how we create, communicate and express ideas and feelings through art, music and performance, but what they have to tell is often opaque when it comes to people, things and relationships. Bob Dylan's lyrics usually give us an enigmatic and paradoxical perspective on the world, not a portal into details of his personal life or beliefs.

The paradoxes and enigmas are often evaded because, as Simon Frith (1996) has pointed out, most writings about song lyrics adopt a realist position, assuming a direct relationship between lyric and an event or emotional condition that it describes or represents. And it is often assumed that a song's popularity must equate with public agreement with its message, allowing Dylan to be characterized (and caricatured) as a "spokesman for a generation" or "voice of the counter-culture".

Dylan's lyrics are far more than the words of a biography or events in a society. It is the composite way that songs are created from multiple experiences and influences combined with large doses of imagination that makes songwriting such a fascinating art. Songs are not in any obvious way about the transmission of details from an artist's life. Songs spring out of the imagination. Songs can come from dreams, from the unfathomable and from somewhere else. Yet they are also composed, put together in a quite deliberate way. Like his music, Dylan draws his words from a variety of sources, songwriting styles and poetic traditions.

Bards, beats, Bogart and the Bible

Literary critics have perhaps inevitably sought out and emphasized the way Dylan's song lyrics seem to make reference to the high literary tradition. Nicholas Roe has provided a list of "just a few" writers and literary influences that have been detected in Dylan's songs:

> W. H. Auden, James Baldwin, William Blake, the Bible, Bertolt Brecht, André Breton, Robert Browning, William Burroughs, Lord Byron, Albert Camus, Joseph Conrad, Gregory Corso, Hart Crane, Leonardo Da Vinci, Charles Dickens, John Donne, T. S. Eliot, William Faulkner, F. Scott Fitzgerald, the French Symbolists, Allen Ginsberg, the Gothic novel, Robert Graves, Greek tragedy, Arthur Hallam, Hamlet, Ernest Hemingway, Hermann Hesse, Geoffrey Hill, Homer, James Joyce, Carl Jung, Franz Kafka, Jack Kerouac, Arthur Koestler, F. R. Leavis, Louis MacNeice, Norman Mailer, Andrew Marvell, John Milton, Friedrich Nietzsche, Thomas Pynchon, John Crowe Ransom, Arthur Rimbaud, Christine Rossetti, Carl Sandburg, Scandina-

vian epics, Scottish ballads, William Shakespeare, John Skelton, John Steinbeck, Dylan Thomas, Henry David Thoreau, twelfth-century troubadours, François Villon, Walt Whitman, W. B. Yeats, and Yevgeny Yevtushenko. (Roe 2003: 85)

You don't have to look far to find other names that might be added to this list (Anton Chekhov or Henry Timrod, for example). Lists like this arise from and encourage a type of obsessive literary detective work, with analysts finding or inventing ever more obscure or fleeting influences.

Roe uses his list for yet another variant on the theme of the Bob Dylan mask, arguing that Dylan "is apparently most himself as a sublimely capable alias, merged into a babel of other's voices" (*ibid.*). Yet, Dylan's voice has been one of the most distinct in popular music. Far from being submerged in a babble of other voices, he has, like so many original artists, found an individual style by drawing from a few very specific poets and songwriters. Dylan may have occasionally name-checked various literary figures in some of his songs, but many of the literary connections (as identified in the list above) are passing or tenuous. It is, after all, easy to spot the musical and lyrical influence of the blues and folk – it is readily apparent in Dylan's verses, phrases, lines, vocal style, instrumentation, rhyme and rhythm, melodies and chords. It is not so easy to hear any direct reference to most of these literary figures. Even Rimbaud is in the background rather than a direct influence. As Dave Van Ronk recalled in memoirs of his time in the folk scene with Dylan:

> Somewhere in my bookcases I probably still have a paperback collection of modern French poetry with Bobby's underlinings in it. I have never traced any of the underlinings to anything he actually used in a song, but he was reading that stuff very carefully. (2006: 207)

The most significant formative and recurrent literary influence on Dylan's songwriting and performing style is that of beat poetry, although even this clear source is by no means as prevalent as the poetics of folk, blues and country. Dylan drew inspiration from the attitude and ambience created by the writings of Jack Kerouac, the poetry of Gregory Corso and most significantly by Allen Ginsberg's poetry (particularly Ginsberg's 'Howl').

The term "beat" initially referred to someone who was down and out, poor or dead-beat. It soon acquired other resonances – upbeat, beatific, on the beat. Stylistically, the beat poets looked to black culture for inspiration, drawing on the street style, gestures, art, argot, rhythms and music of "the Negro Hipster" (Whaley 2004). Beat poetry romanticized while at the same time it sought to demystify the lives of the downtrodden and dispossessed. The homeless, petty thieves, hustlers, prostitutes, pimps, junkies, the mentally ill, marginalized artists, nocturnal workers and itinerant musicians became metaphoric figures, employed poetically to convey displacement and alienation from establishment norms and values (Whaley 2004). The influence of the French Symbolist poets Rimbaud, Baudelaire and Verlaine was also strongly mediated to Dylan via the beats, not only in how they used words but in their adoption of a bohemian lifestyle that sought inspiration in North Africa and embraced drugs as enhancers of reality and stimulators of artistic discovery. The visionary imagery of William Blake also came to Dylan, at least initially, via Ginsberg's poetry.

Beat poetry was performed in the cafes and the clubs of San Francisco and New York's Greenwich Village, often accompanied by experimental or free jazz musicians. It emphasized the incantatory quality of words as rhythmic sound that could be chanted, the words often working as fragmentary, pulsing sonic symbols rather than fully formed semantic statements. Rhythmically, the performed poetry was influenced by the pace and energy of bebop, along with patterns of street speech and slang. Ginsberg brought to this the discernible influence of Jewish cantillation, a form of ritual chanting, in his hypnotic pulsing intonation. He was particularly adept at chanting poems, often performing with little or no amplification in venues where audiences would find it difficult to hear the fine semantic nuances of the poems.

Using provocative juxtapositions, down-to-earth imagery, and words simply for their sounds, the beat poets accented the absurdity and futility of life, the pathos and tragedy of people on the margins. For a brief period in the mid-1960s Dylan went further into the realms of the absurd and grotesque. The influence of the beats can be heard in the way he "painted freaks and geeks" to convey a sense of "grotesques in everyday life" (Shelton 1986: 268), populating his songs on *Highway 61 Revisited* with a macabre carnival of characters such as Dr Filth, the sword-swallower, a one-eyed midget, bandits, Gypsy Davey with a blowtorch, Mack the Finger, and Einstein disguised as Robin Hood. Shelton likened these characters to "medieval gargoyles on Notre Dame" and "types in Rimbaud and Apollinaire" and found them "distantly related to tortured figures in the paintings of Goya, Velázquez, Bosch, and Callot" (*ibid.*: 267). That term "distantly related" might apply to many of the connections between Dylan's lyrics and European art or literature. Whether or not Dylan was drawing on high art and Symbolist poetry, he was explicitly using imagery from circuses and carnivals, alluding to the freak show, and from his immersion in folk and blues. He had clearly picked up on "grotesque and surreal traits" in the songs of Robert Johnson along with a strand of the gothic and grotesque that threads through many old ballads (Ford 1998; Godu 1995; Marcus 1997).

In juxtaposing imagery from different sources in his songwriting, Dylan has consistently used a vocabulary derived from the Bible. Biblical imagery has been a pervasive presence as narrators and characters in Dylan's songs search for but never find some form of redemption. Gray has argued that "the quest for salvation might well be the central theme of his entire output" (2006: 80). Here again, mixed with biblical allusion, is the influence of the blues, and particularly the imagery of Robert Johnson, whose "vision was a world without salvation, redemption or rest; it was a vision he resisted, laughed at, to which he gave himself over, but most of all it was a vision he pursued" (Marcus 1977: 24). Time and time again in Dylan's lyrical imagery, there is no feeling of personal fulfilment, no redemption from a world of strife, estrangement, alienation and disaffection. There are only temporary moments of reprieve in the arms of women or, for a very brief period, in the teachings of Jesus – the albums *Slow Train Coming* and *Saved* marking the only times when Dylan has used the Bible as a literal message of faith, rather than for its allegorical possibilities.

Dylan may include extensive biblical references in a single song, as in the hymn-like, confessional 'Every Grain Of Sand', which, according to Gray (2000: 402), draws from Psalm 119, and also from the books of Luke, Isaiah, Daniel, Mark and Matthew, although its tone is indebted to William Blake's 'Auguries of Innocence', which begins "to see a world in a grain of sand". Or Dylan may use more subtle, passing biblical references, as in the use of the loaded image of the "crown of thorns" in 'Shelter From The Storm' or "this is the day only the Lord can make" in 'The Levee's Gonna Break'. The biblical allusions are incorporated in the manner adopted by numerous blues and gospel musicians, as a way of explaining the present – the narrator's experience either of being treated as a martyr (with a "crown of thorns") or of flooding beyond human control or influence (only the Lord can create such a thing). Dylan's biblical imagery, strongly influenced by its use in the blues, is also a legacy of the way spirituals used the Bible for dramatic and moral effect. Robert Darden has written that

> perhaps the greatest lyrical gift of the spirituals may have been their unknown composers' extraordinary ability to transform the heroes (and villains) of the Bible into a shared experience that not only taught theology but created a universal literature, an ethical model, and a method of disseminating information as well as providing a precious few moments of respite and entertainment and a source of succour to the afflicted and abused. (2004: 84)

Dylan drew on the way the Bible had been incorporated into the poetics of spirituals, folk ballads and blues – a vernacular rather than a high-art influence and one that pervades the songs on *John Wesley Harding*, which quote extensively from the Bible when summoning a sparse landscape populated by shadowy drifters and "damsels", itinerants and immigrants, outlaws and outcasts. 'All Along The Watchtower' takes much of its imagery from Isaiah 21 and briefly references Revelation. Having visited him, Shelton reported that Dylan's study at the time contained "a huge Bible opened on a raised wooden bookstand, and the songs of Hank Williams near at hand" (1986: 389).

A striking example of how Dylan's songwriting connects words from contrasting sources can be found on *Empire Burlesque*, where he combines "the language of Hollywood and of the Bible, the language of movies and of scripture" (Gray 2000: 561). The 1941 film *The Maltese Falcon* is at the core of the album's lyrical imagery (Lindley 1986). Among the quotations from *The Maltese Falcon* that are integrated into the album are "I don't mind a reasonable amount of trouble", a line spoken by Sam Spade (the character played by Humphrey Bogart) that features in 'Seeing The Real You At Last'; this song also contains a slight variation on another Sam Spade line, "I'll have some rotten nights after I've sent you over, but that'll pass". Dylan takes another two of Spade's remarks, "I don't care who loves who" and "All

we've got is that maybe you love me and maybe I love you", and links them
up in 'When The Night Comes Falling From The Sky'. The album quotes from
other films featuring Bogart, including the phrase "There's some people you
don't forget even if you've only seen them once", from *The Big Sleep* and
used in 'I'll Remember You', and "Think this rain would cool things off, but
it don't", which appears in *Key Largo* and is slightly modified in 'Seeing The
Real You At Last'. 'When The Night Comes Falling From The Sky' not only
references numerous movies but starts with the line "Look out across the
fields, see me returning", which echoes John 4:35 (Trager 2004: 677). The
album also uses lines from many other films including *Bronco Billy*, *The
Hustler* and *Shane*.

Biblical and Hollywood references are woven throughout the lyrics of
'Tight Connection To My Heart', which opens with a line derived from
Bogart's character in *Sirocco* who says, "I've got to move fast, I can't with
you around my neck". Later it includes the line "I don't know whether I'm
too good for you or you're too good for me" from the same film and
features dialogue from Bogart in *Tokyo Joe* and an exchange between Bogart's
character Spade and police officers in *The Maltese Falcon*: "We want to talk

At home in Woodstock 1968

to you, Spade", "Well, go ahead and talk". Gray hears the integration of biblical imagery and film dialogue in 'Tight Connection To My Heart' as a way of reflecting on the meaning of the wilderness, evoking the restless wandering that finds resonances in the Song of Solomon ('Song Of Songs'). For Gray the fate of the song's protagonist also parallels that of John the Baptist (Gray 2000: 563). The line "I never could learn to drink that blood, and to call it wine" is a direct reference to the symbolic blood of Christ in the Christian liturgy; the line "what looks large from a distance, close up ain't never that big" has its source in *Now and Forever*, in which Gary Cooper says of the police, "Close up they don't look as large as they do from a distance". The lyrics to *Empire Burlesque* are a typically Dylanesque mixture, created by juxtaposing, synthesizing and contrasting lines, phrases and ideas absorbed or consciously taken from both the sacred and the secular, the elevated and the everyday.

Everyday phrases, lists and rhymes

Dylan grew up absorbing influences from blues, folk, country, rock'n'roll, ballads, standards, vaudeville, pop and show tunes – genres in which songs play on the listener's sense of familiarity and draw on the vocabulary of everyday life. Ordinary words in a song can alert us to the way we use terms and phrases unselfconsciously in our lives, they remind us that we think and speak in unoriginal stock phrases. Some may call them clichés, but they allow us to communicate and can be unobtrusively effective when put into popular song. Words that may seem trite, innocuous and ordinary when read on paper can become profound and extraordinary when sung, *heard* in a totally different way (Frith 1996; Middleton 1990). Dylan has spoken of the everyday sources of his lyrics when talking about songwriting: "You can go anywhere in daily life and have your ears open and hear something, either something someone says to you or something you hear across the room. If it has resonance, you can use it in a song" (Hilburn 2005: 74).

Everyday phrases have been a consistent feature of Dylan's titles. During the 1960s he included such everyday terms as "don't think twice", "one of us must know", "just like a woman", "you go your way and I'll go mine" and "tell me that it isn't true". Into the 1970s and 1980s he sang "you're a big girl now", "if you see her, say hello", "we better talk this over", "seeing the real you at last", "trust yourself". Since the latter half of the 1990s he's used "I'm love sick", "till I fell in love with you", "bye and bye" and "someday baby". Such phrases also crop up everywhere in his lyrics. 'Lay, Lady, Lay', one of his best-known songs, features such apparently banal lines as "his clothes are dirty but his hands are clean" and "you can have your cake and eat it too". The first verse of 'Like A Rolling Stone' reorganizes a series of outbursts that might have been overheard in New York City, the song being acutely attuned to the rhythm of street slang – "you dressed so fine ... you threw the bums a dime ... didn't you? ... now you don't talk so loud ... now you don't seem so proud". Forty years later, on *Modern Times*, he brings a vulnerable, melancholic pathos to a tale of ageing love or friendship when singing the seemingly ordinary line "we live and we die, we know not why" in the song 'When The Deal Goes Down'.

Dylan can be extremely economical with words (*John Wesley Harding*, *Nashville Skyline* and *New Morning*, made between 1967 and 1970, being obvious examples), but he is also notorious for packing lots of lyrics into a song. Rather than selecting a precisely focused, finely polished thought or idea, he'll cram in phrases that at first seem ungainly or incongruous, leaving their rough edges exposed, and then he will skilfully deliver them in such a way as to make them essential to the song, their literary flaws irrelevant. For example, in 'Disease Of Conceit' he manages to get away with this: "Conceit is a disease, but the doctors got no cure, they've done a lot of research on it, but what it is they're still not sure." As Robert Christgau first wrote in 1967, when responding both to the idea that Dylan is a poet and to the economical and pared-down *John Wesley Harding*:

> He has never hesitated to fill the meter with a useless word or to wrench tone in the service of rhyme. Much of his best work is simply too long ... Despite all the talk about "poetry", Dylan has always been a word-crazy dramatist; his "images" are mostly situations full of incongruities and awkward in syntax and diction. (2004: 66)

Even Liam Clancy, who admitted that he wasn't really convinced by Dylan until he heard him sing 'A Hard Rain's A-Gonna Fall', voiced his reservations about this: "I heard him sing it, and I told him, 'Bobby, you have a great gift. Those wonderful words just flow out of you. But do there have to be so many of them? All those verses!'" (Hajdu 2002: 119). Many of Dylan's songs gain their power and persuasiveness from a relentless accumulation of images, ideas and observations, making it almost impossible to take in the full range of allusions and associations in one hearing.

Dylan is particularly adept at playing with and varying the density of what Dai Griffiths (2003) has called the "verbal space" of the song – the time available to deliver lyrics as the song unfolds. Griffiths gives the example 'The Groom's Still Waiting At The Altar', a 12-bar blues which contains a verse that begins with a ten-syllable line, "Cities on fire, phones out of order", and ends with the line "She could be respectably married, or running a whorehouse in Buenos Aires". The lyrics are delivered in the same time, but within one verse Dylan has doubled the "syllabic density within the line" (*ibid.*: 47). Like so many song lyrics, regardless of genre, Dylan's words may look unwieldy or clumsy; beginnings or endings may seem arbitrary. As lines of "poetry" on a page they may seem fragmented, directionless and inconclusive. It is this quality of Dylan's songs that poses such a challenge to other musicians. Dylan sings his songs – rhythmically, melodically, and semantically – as someone who lives and literally breathes the song into existence. His characteristic vocal "authority" (Marshall 2007) becomes all the more obvious when lesser singers attempt to cover his songs.

Dylan uses rhyme constantly, sometimes obsessively, and it is fundamental to the rhythm and dynamics of his songs. He uses the qualities of vowels and consonants to give melodic emphasis, rhythmic accent and to create tension or movement, rhyming with and to the beat, or in anticipation of or slightly behind the beat. In the epic 'It's Alright, Ma (I'm Only Bleeding)', a torrent of rapid rhymes end each pithy line – "noon/ spoon/ balloon/ moon/ soon … fates/ waits/ plates/ gates/ United States". These propel the song forward, adding urgency to the singer's personal anxiety and public disgust at the corruption and conceit that surround him. In 'No Time To Think' the accumulation of ever more weighty single rhymes adds to the cluttered, claustrophobic circumstances that give him no pause for thought – "paradise, sacrifice, mortality, reality … equality, liberty, humility, simplicity … socialism, hypnotism, patriotism, materialism".

Again, words that might appear incongruous on paper can be rhymed in performance as a way of creating unusual poetic associations. Among the many examples in 'The Groom's Still Waiting At The Altar' Dylan rhymes "January" with "Buenos Aires" and "humiliated" with "obligated". *Blood On*

The Tracks contains numerous skilfully sung and instantly memorable rhymes, just one example being "Idiot wind, blowing like a circle around my skull, from the Grand Coulee Dam to the Capitol". In his early knockabout 'I Shall Be Free', he even manages to slip in wry rhymes of "June, moon, spoon".

Dylan is also a notoriously listing songwriter. He'll identify an issue, a theme, an experience, or an event and he'll then build up an impression of it through a list of characteristics, from the list of things seen, sounds heard and people met by his "blue-eyed son" in 'A Hard Rain's A-Gonna Fall', to the list of absurd characters in 'Desolation Row', from the list of adorable attributes of his lover in 'Sad-Eyed Lady Of The Lowlands' to the list of fruit fillings in 'Country Pie'. In later songs we encounter the circumstances and ideas that give him 'No Time To Think', the people and professions who 'Gotta Serve Somebody', and a list of damage done in 'Everything Is Broken'.

Lists work well because song lyrics, by their very nature, are "iterative" (Booth 1981), based on the repetition of ideas, phrases, stanzas, hooks, themes. This is particularly so in folk and blues and allows singers to omit verses or deliver stanzas in different sequences and still convey the emotion and meaning of a song. In concert Dylan has sometimes dropped or resequenced verses or lines, as folk singers have been doing for centuries – and Gray has vociferously complained about it. Pouncing on the way Dylan has dropped verses from 'Jokerman' and 'Desolation Row', Gray moralizes about Dylan's "shrugging-off of the task of full performance", calling it a "short-changing of the audience" and "in essence another expression of self-contempt" (2000: 855). Far from being a lazy "short-changing" of the audience, these edits may be heard as ways of making the songs more effective as musical performances, not least when delivered alongside other songs and within the overall length, pacing, flow and dynamics of an evening's set. Rather than acting in self-contempt, the resequencing and dropping of verses is indicative of a musician who is adapting songs to circumstances and giving the audience more songs in the time available, not short-changing them. As Lee Marshall (2007) has also written, in picking up on this point, many members of the audience, hearing the songs as music at a show, don't notice the dropped verses anyway.

Stories in songs

Like many great songwriters Dylan is a storyteller, populating his songs with characters (often troubled, rarely fulfilled) and using a repertoire of narrative ploys to convey plot and punchline or, more often than not, to leave things open, ambiguous and unresolved. Here again literary critics have made some grand claims when it comes to Dylan and narrative. Several writers have jumped to the conclusion that his song lyrics provide examples of modernist techniques of narrative disruption, juxtaposition and collage. Day is typical when he claims that many lyrics "characteristically display a difficulty and an opacity, a dislocation of common sense". According to Day, it is here in these lyrics that "display disruptions – to varying degrees and in various kinds – of rational order and logical sequence that Dylan's work reveals a cardinal inheritance from the practices of classic modernist poetry" (1988: 3–4).

Arguments like this (and Day is not alone) give an entirely misleading impression of where Dylan draws his inspiration, "reading" Dylan from the standpoint of novels and drama rather than oral poetry and song. Again it is an attempt to align Dylan with a high cultural tradition, but his narrative sources are far more vernacular. Gray has made exactly this point when observing that this apparently modernist feature "is surely the same 'disturbance of narrative order' achieved unselfconsciously by that unmodern form, the narrative ballad". Gray goes on to point out that ballads present a

> world where people disappear and reappear unexpectedly, communication is rife with lethal error and people wear the masks of alias. They are typical too in switching, often without clarification, from one narrator's voice to another, from one situation and location to another and back again, and into the realm where "I", "she" and "you" are well-nigh indecipherably split. (2000: 380)

If pre-modern ballads such as 'Barbara Allen' or 'The Unfortunate Rake' display "random journeys of memory, the non-sequential nature of brooding and remembrance" (*ibid.*), so do modern pop songs. There is nothing particularly unusual or modernist about the words of popular songs defying rational order and logical sequence, or in moving between viewpoints or in rapidly shifting from past to present or future, nor in the use of what might be perceived as juxtaposition or jump-cut. Dylan's contemporaries the Beatles used such techniques constantly, right from 'She Loves You', in which the minimal lyrics move rapidly between present, past and the present (future) in the past.

Betsy Bowden has emphasized this characteristic of Dylan's songwriting, treating it as a legacy of the performed song tradition (rather than modernist poetry). Referring to 'Just Like A Woman', she describes how Dylan "writing for oral performance, has disallowed the words any linear progression in time. The narrative situation jerks from 'Tonight' to 'lately' to 'finally' to 'the

On stage at Blackbushe Aerodrome, England, 1978

first' to 'When we meet again'" (2001: 56). The lyrical content wanders between present, past and future and "any attempt to figure out exactly who said and did what, in what order, is inappropriate – for this is a song not a poem" (*ibid.*). Another example is 'Just Like Tom Thumb's Blues', a song with no recurring chorus in which "Dylan switches back and forth between the first, second and third person until it's far from clear who's singing, who's being sung to and who's being sung about" (Williamson 2004: 272).

If narrative is a way of telling a story, and the story is all the events depicted, and the plot is the causal chain of connections that link these events, then it is clear that popular songs narrate the world in a very different way from drama or novels. Novels unfold over considerable time as read, whereas songs unfold over short periods of time as heard. Songs are sung with repeated hooks or choruses being integral to their plot or punchline, with melody and rhythm contributing to a listener's comprehension of narrative sequence, occurrence and recurrence. Bridging the distinction between the real and imaginary, crossing back and forth between self and character, songs allow singers to narrate stories in a way that can emphasize the very fact that life (unlike most novels, movies and plays) doesn't seem to have much of a plot for most of the time anyway. Movements between narrators and addressee, between past, present and future, and a lack of plot or resolution are characteristics of song as a form. As Mark Booth concluded in his study of songs ranging from ancient ballads to advertising jingles, "even narrative song tends towards tableau" (1981: 163). Songs are closer to the way stories are conveyed in the visual arts than on the printed page.

One clear visual influence on Dylan's songwriting is cinema. It is impossible to exaggerate the impact of movies on perception and behaviour since the 1920s. Film changed the way people saw themselves and others: the dramatic impact of the close-up on a huge screen (at more or less the same time during the 1930s when the microphone was providing an intimate close-up of a singer's voice); the exaggerated movement of people and things; the new types of visual narrative that were developed to convey time passing or to move between past and present. The cinema influenced novelists, painters and songwriters. The themes, structure and narrative tricks of Dylan's songwriting have constantly been informed by a "cinematic imagination" (Mellers 1984; Shelton 1986) and can be heard in 'Motorpsycho Nitemare',

'Bob Dylan's 115th Dream', 'Hurricane', 'Black Diamond Bay', and 'Brownsville Girl'. Even the finger-pointing 'The Lonesome Death Of Hattie Carroll' conveys the story as a pictorial tableau or series of episodes rather than a straight narrative.

Perhaps *the* Bob Dylan song that has been cited most frequently in discussions of narrative is 'Tangled Up In Blue', one of his most popular and much-performed songs. Starting with an ordinary, familiar phrase that has featured in numerous folk ballads and blues – "early one morning" – the song takes the listener through a series of tableaux that sketch different relationships, encounters and events, combined with reflections about growing older, looking back and moving on. Dylan deliberately composed the song to defy any single or one-dimensional interpretation. He had been studying painting with Norman Raeben and was interested in representing different experiences of time and perspective. In one interview he said, "I was just trying to make it like a painting, where you can see the different parts but then you also see the whole of it" (Williams 1992: 23). Elsewhere he explained, "I wanted to defy time, so that the story took place in the present and the past at the same time. When you look at a painting, you can see any part of it, or see all of it together. I wanted that song to be like a painting" (Heylin 2000: 370).

'Tangled Up In Blue' has attracted a lot of interpretation, particularly from those seeking biographical clues and not least because it featured on *Blood On The Tracks*, when it was known that Dylan's marriage was in difficulty. Yet, as Oliver Trager cautions, "Interpreting this song is a rather slippery slope. Is Dylan describing the arc of a single obsessive relationship? Several couples' itinerant meetings and breakups? Or one man's relationship with many women?" (2004: 605).

Dylan has compounded the ambiguities during live performances by constantly changing the personal pronouns, sometimes altering small details, occasionally modifying complete scenes, and often dropping a verse (most frequently, but not always, the one in which a woman opens up a book of poems). A mere hint of these variations can be gained by listening to the versions that appear on *Blood On The Tracks*, *The Bootleg Series Volume 5. Bob Dylan Live 1975* and *Real Live* (there are, of course, numerous versions on bootleg recordings of gigs). In concert the song has opened with "Early one morning the sun was shining, I was laying in bed" and "... he was laying in bed" and "... she was laying in bed"; the song has been delivered from the perspective of the first person ("our lives") and third person ("their lives"). Minor modifications have included a change of occupations (from working as a "cook" to working "in an old hotel"; from "carpenter" to "truck driver"). In November 1978, instead of opening up a book of poems by a thirteenth-century Italian poet, the woman opened up the Bible (Williams 1992), a change interpreted (in retrospect) as an indication of Dylan's impending Christian period. The most striking rewrite is the version that appears on *Real Live*, in which Dylan substitutes more direct language, drawing phrases from everyday speech, using a less overtly poetic vocabulary (in keeping with a general shift in his lyric writing during the mid-1980s).

Dylan's voices

The lack of a definitive version of 'Tangled Up In Blue' is once again a reminder that Dylan's lyrics do not appear as poetry or words arranged neatly on a page. He sings them. The different versions of this song also highlight the importance of Dylan's voices – not only have the words been changed, but they have been sung in subtly different ways, the events recounted by Dylan as a more detached observer or the situations inflected with a mood of personal nostalgia. Dylan's performing voice always intervenes in the narrative, bridging, blurring and confusing the distinction between the character in a lyric and the persona of Bob Dylan.

Like all unique vocal stylists, Dylan spent a lot of time listening to other singers and experimenting with voices that allowed him to express his character and convey the sentiments of songs. Shelton quotes Spider John Koerner, who knew Dylan when he was performing in coffee-houses in Minneapolis; "Dylan had a very sweet voice, a pretty voice, much different from what it became" (1986: 66). You can hear him still searching for a voice, or a repertoire of voices, throughout his first album *Bob Dylan*, on which he occasionally verges on rural folk pastiche and veers towards some theatrical overstated performances, particularly when he's forcing the blues feeling in 'Fixin' To Die' and 'Highway 51'. But it is the nasal timbre and bluesy approach to breathing, phrasing and intonation that run like a thread through Dylan's singing from this first album, where the voices of other blues singers are a phantom presence, such as 'In My Time Of Dyin'' (Blind Willie Johnson) or 'Fixin' To Die' (Bukka White), through to the melismatic gypsy blues of 'One More Cup Of Coffee' in the mid-1970s, and up to the softer, relaxed, semi-spoken style of 'Thunder On The Mountain' in 2006.

Since he started singing, many have commented, often disparagingly, about Dylan's voice. In 1964 the novelist John Updike notoriously described it as a "voice you could scour a skillet with". A year later, the poet Philip Larkin distilled it as "cawing, derisive", whilst in 1971 David Bowie called it "a voice like sand and glue" in his 'Song For Bob Dylan' on the album *Hunky Dory* (1971).

Yet, right from Dylan's first album it is quite clear that he does not simply have a voice, singular. By the end of the 1960s it was surely even more obvious. The declamatory protest singer on much of *The Times They Are A-Changin'* or the raucous blues singer on *Bringing It All Back Home* and *Highway 61 Revisited* may well have the "sand and glue" or "cawing, derisive" quality, but not the intimate drawl permeating *Blonde On Blonde*, or the understated chronicler's voice on *John Wesley Harding* or the romantic country croon on *Nashville Skyline*. Like many vocalists, Dylan's singing is limited by what physiology has made possible, it is self-consciously stylized and mannered, and has become cracked and raspy as he has aged. But the distinct vocal styles he developed cannot be so simply characterized or caricatured.

Not only has Dylan changed his singing style over time, he has used his voice to accommodate, convey, comment upon or even challenge the circumstances, character and sentiment implied in specific lyrics. The lyric may lead the voice, but the voice can lead the lyric astray, imposing upon it, subverting or transforming the apparent meaning. 'Positively 4th Street', for example, a song dealing with the betrayal of friendship, has been delivered as an indignant, withering put-down and also as a melancholic, regretful lament. A number of writers have commented on how the lyrics of 'Just Like A Women', interpreted as misogynistic on paper, have often become far more ambivalent when delivered in a sensitive, intimate, understated, sometimes melancholic manner. The meaning of the song arises from the interplay and tension that Dylan sets up between voice and lyric, a quality of songs in performance that Frith emphasized and illustrated in *Performing Rites* (1996).

Very early in the 1960s Dylan adopted a *moralizing voice*, a feature of his finger-pointing and consciousness-raising songs. This can be heard on such songs as 'Only A Pawn In Their Game' and 'With God On Our Side', accenting the words, emphasizing the message in a strident, occasionally preaching and judgemental manner. It is a voice that draws stylistically from folk and blues. It is an orator's voice, addressing the public, in part required by or provoked by the lyrics and the need to get them heard at the time. But it is a voice that Dylan grew tired of and renounced in 'My Back Pages', although it lurks within the accusatory delivery of 'Ballad Of A Thin Man' and 'Hurricane' and occasionally surfaces during the evangelical preaching performances on *Saved* and during the gospel concerts of 1979–80, and even occasionally during later performances of 'Masters Of War'.

Dylan has also used a more subtle *observation* or *narrative voice*, drawing on a long tradition of song as story, part of a broader tradition of oral storytelling. Dylan's narrative voice shapes itself to the words, directly informing the melodic and rhythmic contour of the song, and often verges on or becomes the intonation of speech, sometimes half-sung, half-spoken, as in 'Brownsville Girl' or 'T.V. Talkin' Song'. This voice also adopts a similar intonation to that used in spoken dialogue when conveying the narrator's or a character's emotion – joy in 'If Not For You', anger in 'Idiot Wind', romantic awe in 'Angelina' or impatience in 'What Was It You Wanted?'

Dylan has adopted a softer *intimate voice* when expressing tenderness, vulnerability, love or regret. It is there on his second album, *The Freewheelin' Bob Dylan*, concurrent with his protest singing, and can be heard on 'Girl From The North Country' and 'Don't Think Twice, It's All Right' and a little later on 'One Too Many Mornings'. This is a voice that Dylan will perfect on *Blonde On Blonde*, where he sings some of his most intimate songs, with a calm, casual drawl, intoning close to the microphone, rarely pitching the melodies where he has to strain for blues effect – 'One Of Us Must Know (Sooner or Later)', 'Visions Of Johanna', 'I Want You' and 'Sad-Eyed Lady Of The Lowlands'. The intimate voice, influenced by the country folk ballad and softly crooned popular song, was a prominent feature of *Nashville Skyline* and continued through songs on *Blood On The Tracks*, *Empire Burlesque* and up to 'When The Deal Goes Down' on *Modern Times*.

Dylan has an *externalizing voice*, which he uses for the outward expression of an inner sensation. This is a voice he adopts to convey a mood of internal anxiety, confusion, or an emotional dilemma. The voice appears to reach out from the inside, from the deeply personal; it then usually becomes public before returning to the inside. The melodies often appear to arc – to rise and fall – suddenly or gradually; the singing voice tenses, reaches out and up towards the higher pitches and then relaxes and returns inward. Vocal melodies that use rising pitches have come to be associated with a more active and outgoing identity, whereas falling pitches are indicative of more inward or introspective qualities (Middleton 1990; Van Leeuwen 1999). The externalizing voice becomes pronounced just over half-way through the fourth album, *Another Side Of Bob Dylan*. After the opening seven songs, 'My Back Pages' appears and suddenly signals a more soul-searching singer. There is a sense of liberation, a looseness to the voice that is freeing itself from expectations. Gray has remarked that Dylan's voice actually starts to *sound* younger on this song. A similar mood is apparent on 'It Ain't Me, Babe', when the voice reaches out and up, hurls the words out into the world – "I was so much older then" or "No, no, no, it ain't me, babe" – and then relaxes, comes down, returns to the self – "I'm younger than that now" or "It ain't me you're lookin' for, babe". There are many other songs where Dylan uses his voice to express an internal state ('Mr. Tambourine Man', 'What Good Am I?', 'Love Sick', for example).

Related to this is an *elegiac voice*, conveying sorrow and offering consolation, a quality that John Hinchey (1989) heard becoming more prominent in Dylan's songwriting during the 1980s, notably on 'Every Grain Of Sand' and characterizing much of *Empire Burlesque*. It is a voice that can be traced right back to 'Song To Woody' on Dylan's first album, but it became more nuanced during the early 1980s when he was conveying the weight of hardship, the loss of innocence or betrayal of cherished beliefs, or when reflecting on mortality, things lost, times gone or slipping away. It is a voice he uses when standing back from relationships in the world, in contrast to singing from the inside. It can be heard on his laments 'Lenny Bruce' and 'Blind Willie McTell' and is a strong thread woven from *Empire Burlesque* through to *Oh Mercy* and *Time Out Of Mind*. It is a voice informed by the lyrics of the songs, but it is also integral to Dylan's vocal style during this period, his voice shaping the lyrics with a more relaxed, deeper and lower (literally low-key) tonality. It is a voice that begins to be used in concert, radically altering the mood of 'Mr. Tambourine Man', for example, and it comes to dominate in many of Dylan's performances after 2003, where

numbers once heard as moralizing "protest songs" become sombre, reflective, low-key lamentations.

Finally, in stark contrast, Dylan has used a frivolous, *jokey voice*, singing
with a laugh in his throat, on such songs as 'I Shall Be Free' or 'Rainy Day
Women # 12 & 35' or the drinking song 'Please Mrs. Henry'. The singing
is more conversational, a raconteur's voice, often more excited, but it
disappeared from official recordings after the 1960s. When the witticisms
finally returned in 2001 with *"Love And Theft"* the humour was delivered
in a more deadpan manner (on 'Po' Boy', for example), or with a degree of
ambiguity, begging the question of whether he is joking or serious or both
simultaneously (a precursor being 'Highlands', the last track on *Time Out Of
Mind* from 1997).

During the first half of the 1960s, Dylan used humour to break up the
seriousness and intensity of albums such as *Freewheelin'* and *Another Side
Of Bob Dylan*, usually mixing musical jokes with lyrical puns and put-ons. In
later years, the deadpan puns and witticisms have been incorporated in a less
conspicuous, wry and ironic manner, adroitly blended into the music, maybe
unnoticed on a casual listen, particularly on *"Love And Theft"*. It is at these
moments, when Dylan is *singing* a joke, with music and rhythm, that it is
more than clear that he is a musician before he is ever a poet.

5 Music

Writing about his songs in *Chronicles: Volume One*, Dylan made this observation:

> For sure my lyrics had struck nerves that had never been struck before, but if my songs were about the words, then what was Duane Eddy, the great rock-and-roll guitarist, doing recording an album full of instrumental melodies of my songs? Musicians have always known that my songs were about more than just words, but most people are not musicians. (2004: 119–20)

Not only do musicians know that the songs are about more than words, so do the audiences who sing along with Dylan at concerts or with recordings, or with songs in their head as they walk down the street. The fans applauding his harmonica solos, and those who dance, know that the songs are music in motion before they are words on a page.

Dylan's wordplay is clearly important. Yet the obsessive lyric-sifters frequently manage to discuss his songs with barely a mention of his voices and vocal gestures, let alone obvious musical characteristics such as melody, rhythm, chords, texture and timbre. Despite their opening caveats (acknowledging that they are dealing with songs), it is soon apparent when reading Christopher Ricks or Michael Gray (to cite the most prominent) that they are obsessed with lyrical detective work (locating sources, making connections) and interpreting the words of the pop song narrowly in terms of semantics.

Many authors acknowledge that the songs are more than words, but then conveniently forget this so that they can discuss the lyrics set out on the page. I will cite one example as an indication of the reasoning and rhetorical sleight of hand that occurs here. Michael Gilmour (2004) sets out to understand the significance of the Bible in Dylan's songs. When explaining his approach he refers to the following comment by Dylan: "Some people, when it comes to me, extrapolate only the lyrics from the music. But, ... the music has just as far-reaching effect" (Gilmour: 7). Gilmour cites Dylan talking about how people neglect the performance and the "feel" of the music. He then decides to ignore the views that he's just quoted, and patronizingly continues: "But with all due respect to the songwriter ... we will focus on the written word in this book" (*ibid.*). He then explains why he prefers to do this, using a type of reasoning that is typical of writers who dissect Dylan's lyrics: "One advantage of the written format is that the reader has the opportunity to slow down, reflect, and cross-reference in a way that the recorded songs do not permit, much less the live performance of a song in concert" (*ibid.*). Such an approach completely misunderstands how the popular song works its magic. Songs are not something we read slowly on a page, reflecting and cross-referencing as we go. Songs unfold as music in time, connecting with our bodies in a manner far removed from the intellectual contemplation and reflection implied here.

Related problems are apparent in Aidan Day's *Jokerman*, subtitled "reading the lyrics of Bob Dylan". Although he acknowledges the prominence of Dylan's voice, he dismisses its musical significance in these terms:

> Typically, the voice engages the line of the melody but its simultaneous jarring, atonal separation from the music, together with the relentless subordination of musical elements to the exigencies of verbal order, opens a space which registers a distance and an unease involving both singer and listener. The singing voice at once solicits and rebuffs. The gratifications it offers are uncomfortable ones. (Day 1988: 2)

To claim that music is subordinate to verbal order is inaccurate and misleading. It is far more likely that the words in Dylan's songs are frequently chosen (or edited during songwriting) to suit the music. This is apparent from accounts of Dylan's recording sessions (Heylin 2000) and from listening to officially available and unofficially distributed recordings of studio out-takes and rehearsals. Dylan's words often work as sounds, being used for their phonetic, rhythmic and evocative character rather than their semantic or representational qualities, for the sonorous quality of the rhymes within the music. Or, as Dylan commented when referring to 'Everything Is Broken',

"The semantic meaning is all in the sounds of the words" (2004: 173-4) – a point the reading literary scholars often seem unable to hear.

Day refers to the "atonal separation" of the vocal melody from the music. As far as I'm aware, all of Dylan's songs have a clear tonal centre, all melodies work in relation to more or less distinct keys, scales or modes, and I cannot hear the voice deviating from this. So, I'll assume that Day is using the term "atonal" in an inaccurate way, to emphasize the idea that Dylan's voice jars on the listener. Now, it is common for those who don't like Dylan to dismiss his voice as grating. Day allows for this opinion because he wants to hear a similar sound, but claim a particular value for it. Drawing on modernist high-art aesthetics (valuing art that seeks to shock, cause difficulty, challenge expectations), Day argues that Dylan solicits and rebuffs and offers an "uncomfortable pleasure".

This argument doesn't stand up to the evidence of how Dylan's melodies, rhythms and voices draw us in, how Dylan's songs intimately engage with his listeners. It seems to ignore how the tunes quite cleverly, and occasionally deceptively, using the well-developed rhetoric of the popular song form, draw us in with their many melodic lines and musical hooks. The vast majority of Dylan's songs are about love, loss and human relationships; their melodies and delivery are more likely to encourage closeness than distance. That feeling of intimacy can be experienced at a concert, or when listening to a recording. Many people, both critics and fans, have sought comfort and solace, along with joy and an impulsive freedom, in the songs of Dylan (rather than uncomfortable pleasures).

Betsy Bowden acknowledges this when referring to the way Dylan's songs have resonated with her emotions, spoken directly to her experiences of life and helped her "articulate what kind of a woman I did not want to be" (2001: 54). In *Performed Literature* she argues that the persuasiveness of Dylan's vocal performance arises from his skill as a singer in shifting and sliding between pitches and singing with an irregular metre. In thinking about this, she develops some very detailed analysis of the way Dylan uses his voice, drawing on ideas from the study of orality and performed poetry to show the contrasting sounds and sentiments that the same word can convey, the varied duration of a word in different performances of a song, and the use of accents, phrasing and a range of vocal timbres. Yet Bowden, like Day, is quite dismissive of Dylan's music and the musicality of his voice. She asserts that there is not much for musicologists to say about Dylan's songs and confidently states: "without words most Dylan melodies and chord changes would be boring" (*ibid.*: 1). The melodies could only be judged boring according to a very specific (and unstated) aesthetic of complexity, one that developed during the late-Romantic and early modernist period. These melodies are certainly not boring according to the aesthetics of folk, blues and pop music. Equally, the chords are only boring if you believe what you see in songbooks and not what you hear on recordings and at concerts.

That seemingly simple word – "boring" – is an index of some of the obstacles that those of us studying popular music continually find in our paths. When much high theory confronts popular and folk culture it often reaches the pejorative conclusion that these musics are formally simple and repetitive. Hence, a further assumption is made – this must be boring. Some writers have attempted to challenge this view by arguing that popular culture is just as formally complex as canonical high culture. Christopher Ricks (2003) does this with his detailed analysis of Dylan's lyrics, finding connections to Tennyson, Shakespeare, Rossetti, Blake, the Bible, Homer, amongst others – but not managing a single mention for Lennon and McCartney, the

© Martin Philby/Redferns

On stage in Melbourne 2003

latter point noted by Anthony Quinn (2003) when reviewing Ricks's book *Dylan's Visions of Sin*.

The search for complexity in popular culture, allied to the desire for scholarly legitimacy for such a project within the academy, again leads away from the distinguishing qualities of Dylan's music. We should pay more attention to the pleasures, practices and aesthetic value of repetition and formal simplicity – the way these work for us both as musicians and as listeners. Dylan is firmly within a performed popular song, rather than a "performed literature", tradition and he is a singer of songs way before he is a "poet" to be scrutinized and cross-referenced on the page.

Interviewed about his songwriting, Dylan once said, "The melodies in my mind are very simple, they're very simple, they're just based on music we've all heard growing up" (Zollo 2003: 73). Studies of Dylan might benefit from accounts of the value of simplicity and how Dylan works hard to achieve this, as a contrast to the studies that make his music seem so complicated, complex, elevated and distanced from everyday experience.

Rising and falling

One way of approaching his music is to think about how Dylan's songs convey meaning through the melodic contour of the song, in particular through the use of rising and falling pitch. Anyone who has listened to blues and rock music will be familiar with what has variously been called the "holler", the "shout and fall", or the "tumbling strain". Peter Van der Merwe speculates that the holler is "probably as old as song itself: a series of improvised, constantly varied strains, all descending to the same low point and often to the same figure". He calls it "the true 'endless melody', without any further organizing principle beyond the grouping of the strains into irregular waves, which themselves taper from high to low" (2004: 444).

Although the shout-and-fall pattern may well be ancient, we rarely encounter it in such a regular sequence, more often as part of a song. Being a major pattern in blues, it is prevalent in Dylan (and much blues-inflected rock music). A dramatic rise in pitch followed by a quick drop characterizes songs that entail a tense "affective outpouring", a musical gesture characterized as "self-offering of the body", and then a more relaxed, inward-looking descent (Middleton 1990: 207). This pattern structures 'A Simple Twist Of Fate', a tale of lost love narrated with very little change in pitch until the voice rises in every verse on the words "straight", "freight", "gate", "re-late", "wait", "late", and each time falls in resignation, returning to that inescapable "simple twist of fate" (this shout-and-fall pattern crops up in a number of songs on *Blood On The Tracks*).

There is a more subtle variation in 'My Back Pages', the song in which Dylan renounced his role as public spokesman, signalling his desire to move away from writing songs for causes and to write only for himself. It is in the hook line of "I was so much older then, I'm younger than that now". When he was so much older, the voice tenses and the pitch rises, the emotion is outward. As he feels younger, the singing muscles relax, the pitch falls, and he returns to the inner self rather than the public figure. The first part of 'Cold Irons Bound' is structured around a similar shout and fall: "I'm beginning to hear voices" (rise), "there's no one around" (fall), and then he descends further until he is way down deep in the mist and feeling like he doesn't exist.

A sudden rising and falling pattern is a key feature of Dylan's songs. It is one of the ways he conveys emotion and uses melody to add dynamism and drama to the narrative. A few of the other songs where you can find this pattern to a greater or lesser extent are: 'The Lonesome Death Of Hattie Carroll', 'I Don't Believe You', 'It Ain't Me, Babe', 'Gates Of Eden', 'It's All Over Now, Baby Blue' (a sudden drop of an entire octave when it's all over), 'As I Went Out One Morning', 'Drifter's Escape', 'I'll Be Your Baby Tonight', 'Crash On The Levee (Down In The Flood)', 'Wedding Song', 'You're A Big Girl Now', 'New Pony', 'Solid Rock', 'Driftin' Too Far From Shore', 'What Good Am I?', 'Million Miles', 'Till I Fell In Love With You', 'High Water (For Charley Patton)', 'Rollin' And Tumblin''.

Less abrupt, more subtle and extended patterns of rising and falling pitch can be found throughout Dylan's songs. 'Mr. Tambourine Man' is characterized by constantly descending lines. It is one of Dylan's most original and extraordinary melodies, and a song that unusually for a pop song commences with the chorus and starts on the subdominant (IV) chord of B♭ rather than the dominant or root chord of F. The melody is contained within an octave, using all eight notes of the major diatonic scale, and he starts singing at the highest pitch (F) as he hails his guide, "Hey, Mr. Tambourine Man" and requests "play a song for me". Throughout the song he calls out with the same highest note of the melody, "take me", "I'm ready", until he joyfully proclaims "yes, to dance". The imagery conjured up by weariness, amazement and the singer's dreamlike state constantly cascades downwards, until his declaration to come "following you" is delivered on the lowest pitch of the melody, an octave below the first pitch (F), as if he has reached his decision, calm and contented to follow the Tambourine Man. Elsewhere, in 'One More Cup Of Coffee' the fall in pitch is predictably associated with descending into the valley below. In 'Slow Train', the ominous train is introduced with a slightly hesitant rising of pitch at the end of the phrase, as if signalling a glimpse of Christian hope amongst the despair and disgust within the secular world.

In concert Dylan has often modified the melodic contour of his songs, particularly by introducing an unresolved ascending pitch. This is very obvious on the version of 'Most Likely You Go Your Way And I'll Go Mine' on *Before The Flood*, a recording of his 1974 US tour with the Band. On the studio version, on *Blonde On Blonde*, he sings "You say you love me and you're thinkin' of me, but you know you could be wrong", with the word "wrong" relaxed, somewhat resigned, slightly descending. In the live version the word "wrong" is snarled and declamatory, delivered with a sudden rise in pitch that leaves the word hanging in the air, like an unchecked angry outburst, the word spat out, rising in the air away from the singer.

Some of Dylan's performances during the late 1990s were characterized by a technique (or habit) that some of his more critical fans called "upsinging" – changing the melodic pattern at the end of phrases to ascend when those familiar with the songs expected a descent. Some wrote of this as irritating and speculated as to whether its purpose was to preserve Dylan's voice when he was playing so many gigs a year (Muir 2001), although it would probably be more relaxing for the voice to descend. Upsinging is a way of sending the words out to the audience without claiming them back, propelling them out into the world, without drawing them back into the self. Perhaps it is significant that this often occurred with songs that he had performed many times before, such as 'Blowin' In The Wind' or 'Mr. Tambourine Man', numbers that almost seemed like public property by this time.

Never-ending melodies

Another deceptively simple musical device is the riff, a short rhythmic melodic phrase, often repeated continuously for the duration of a song. Paul

Williams has emphasized the riff as the key to how Dylan's music works, particularly in concert. He writes: "It's all in the riff. That's the secret of Bob Dylan's music ... the riff calls forth the great vocal performances." Of concert performances, he writes: "when ... the band is directed to vamp on the riff for long non-vocal passages, the riff itself starts speaking to the song's listeners as though these were whole new verses of evocative, mind-blowing, Bob-Dylan-in-his-prime lyrics" (2004: xiii). Acknowledging how Dylan has been able to achieve a similar effect through the distinct voices that he gives to harmonica solos, Williams stresses how, on good nights, Dylan is able to do this through the riff.

Not all Dylan's songs are riff-based. But many are, and in these it is the riff that drives the selection and articulation of words with music. As Dylan explained to Bill Flanagan:

> "A lot of times *riffs* will come into my head. And I'll transpose them with the guitar or piano. A lot of times I'll wake up with a certain riff, or it'll come to me during the day. I'll try to get that down, and then the lines will come from that." (1987: 106)

The riff allows the song to form, to take shape; it provides an integral part of the architecture of a song. It is the cyclical, non-goal-directed repetition of musical phrases and verbal sounds that draws us in, allowing us to enter the song. The riff becomes the song, and words and vocal melody are held in tension to the riff, intimated by and implicated in it.

The riff-based character of Dylan's songs has become ever more pronounced and emphasized in live performance, but there are many studio recordings that provide ample evidence of how his songs are built around riffs. A few examples: 'Maggie's Farm' (particularly in concerts during the 1970s and 1980s), 'Outlaw Blues', 'It's Alright, Ma (I'm Only Bleeding)', 'All Along The Watchtower', 'Crash On The Levee (Down In The Flood)' (particularly live), 'New Pony', 'Solid Rock', 'In The Garden' (live), 'Seeing The Real You At Last', 'Everything Is Broken', 'Tweedle Dee & Tweedle Dum', 'Subterranean Home Sick Blues' (live), 'Lonesome Day Blues', 'The Levee's Gonna Break'. The riff shapes the song, and the words are chosen to convey the meaning of the song as it arises from the interplay between vocal and riff.

If Dylan's songs are not based on a riff, then they are, almost without exception, based on a pattern that is usually referred to as strophic – built on a sequence of changing chords that are continually repeated, perhaps with minor variations in the metre, texture or timbre. In principle, this is similar to the repetition and circularity of 12-bar blues patterns. Numerous folk and popular song traditions around the world are strophic.

Strictly speaking, a "strophe" is considered a verse unit or a stanza, and many of Dylan's songs are based on much smaller "loops". So, for example, 'All Along The Watchtower' is based on a single repeated loop of three chords that recur every 3 to 4 seconds; 'Isis' is based on another three-chord sequence repeated every 4 seconds. Other songs may have more obviously strophic sequences; the strophe of 'Man In The Long Black Coat' is composed of two repeated sequences of about 8 to 9 seconds, and a very similar "chorus" of a similar length, before the cycle recommences. The song that originally filled one side of a vinyl LP when *Blonde On Blonde* was first released, 'Sad-Eyed Lady Of The Lowlands', has two verses followed by a chorus, repeated five times. The musical components that make up the continually repeated unit can be represented as [a a b a a b c c d e e]. The full sequence lasts for nearly two minutes before we go around again. Sometimes Dylan will add a short section somewhere in the middle ('Man In The Long Black Coat'), sometimes not ('Sad-Eyed Lady Of The Lowlands').

Recurring strophic patterns, or loops, and repetition are very important in popular songs. You don't have to listen to a song for long to become familiar with its basic structure and melodic shape. The musician or songwriter can use this to draw the listener in, by introducing subtle changes of tempo or texture or by playing with the dynamics of the song. 'Sad-Eyed Lady Of The Lowlands' is a great example of a song in which Dylan used a repeating, cyclical pattern to gradually build intensity through the music, the rather contrived lyrics almost becoming secondary to the emotional narrative of the music. He recorded this song in Nashville with musicians who were used to playing songs that were made for radio and expected it to be finished after about three minutes. While recording they would build for a climax, in anticipation that the song was about to end, and then find that Dylan was beginning yet another verse. The musicians then had to build the song up again, and again, adding something extra each time. It got to the point where they were unsure when the song would end (Sounes 2001: 242). This probably contributes to the vitality and dynamic intensity of this 11-minute performance.

Just as strophic patterns are fundamental to Dylan's songwriting, so too are pentatonic melodies. Formally, a pentatonic scale consists of five notes within the interval of an octave. The most obvious example that is often given is the black notes on the piano; these five notes make up the intervals of a pentatonic scale, and you can pick out various tunes on them, notably 'Auld Lang Syne'. Like many self-taught piano-players Dylan developed a preference for the keys (pitch centres) that contain more of the black notes of the keyboard (such as C♯ or D♭ and D♯ or E♭). The black notes are one of the easiest ways of picking out pentatonic melodies, and I think it is no coincidence that Dylan discussed his songwriting in these terms:

> "On the piano, my favourite keys are the black keys. And they *sound* better on guitar, too ... when you take a black key song and put it on the guitar, which means you're playing in A flat, not too many people like to play in those keys ... the songs that go into those keys right from the piano, they sound different. They sound deeper. Yeah. They sound deeper. Everything sounds deeper in those black keys." (Zollo 2003: 75)

Dylan's view is less to do with any mystical properties of the keys. It is partly a technical issue. He acknowledges that when playing with guitarists it is usually necessary to transpose into a different key (from B♭ to A, or from A♭ to A or G), simply because the chords are harder to finger on the guitar; this creates a different timbre because there are fewer open strings sounding in the flattened chords. Additionally, when playing on just the black notes of the keyboard, or in keys (pitch centres) which contain more black notes, there is a greater tendency to pick out pentatonic melodies. It may be that some of Dylan's "deeper songs" – or the ones he feels are deeper – are based on pentatonic melodies, rather than the more regular diatonic scale. 'Blind Willie McTell' (in *The Bootleg Series Volumes 1–3*), one of Dylan's greatest songs, is pentatonic and sung almost entirely with the black notes of the piano (in the key of E♭/D♯).

Music theorists have tried to classify pentatonic "systems" by identifying recurrent pentatonic scales or modes, comprised of such sequences as C, E♭, F, G, B♭ (minor pentatonic) or C, D, E, G, A (major pentatonic). If you run up and down these notes, you will get a sense of a pentatonic feel (they tend not to use "leading" semitone intervals), but in practice (like the so-called blues scales or blues mode) pentatonic melodies are not based on such systematic and regular sequences. Many of the melodies of Dylan's songs are based on five notes or less, and when occasional extra notes appear they do not detract from a strong pentatonic mood. This is clearly the influence of Dylan's immersion in Delta blues, folk ballad, gospel and the enduring legacy of children's rhymes. Wilfrid Mellers has written that "pentatonic formulae prevail in folk music in all cultures at all stages of evolution and are, indeed, spontaneously uttered by little children, even by those living in complex societies moulded by industrialism, literacy and, in musical terms, by harmonic concepts" (1981: 144). Pentatonic melodies predate the use of standard triadic guitar chords and modern piano tuning, which is another reason why there may be no necessary "functional" relationship between vocal melody lines and chords, and why the interaction between the chord and vocal may be assumed by classically trained musicians to contain "dissonance" (even if not heard as dissonant by musicians or listeners).

On Dylan's first album, recorded in the autumn of 1961, 'Song To Woody' is a pentatonic melody based on the notes A, B, C♯, E, F♯, and it was still the same five note melody, but in G, when he was performing it live during 2000. Forty-five years later, the final song on *Modern Times*, 'Ain't Talkin'', uses a pentatonic melody based on G♯, B, C♯, D♯, F♯, with an occasional slight flattening of the D♯ and very infrequent flattening of the B. In between these recordings are numerous songs that use a clear pentatonic melody, just *some* of these being 'Masters Of War', 'The Ballad Of Hollis Brown', 'She Belongs To Me', 'It's All Over Now, Baby Blue', 'Ballad Of A Thin Man', 'I Dreamed I Saw St Augustine', 'I Am A Lonesome Hobo', 'The Wicked Messenger', 'All The Tired Horses', 'Father Of Night', 'Knockin' On Heaven's Door', 'Dirge', 'Isis', 'Sara', 'Changing Of The Guards', 'Baby Stop Crying', 'Señor (Tales Of Yankee Power)', almost the whole of *Slow Train Coming*, and quite a bit of *Saved*, well over half the songs on *Shot Of Love*, 'I And I', 'Seeing The Real You At Last', 'When The Night Comes Falling From The Sky', 'Dark Eyes', 'Brownsville Girl', most of *Oh Mercy*, not much of *Under The Red Sky*, well over half of *Time Out Of Mind*, 'Things Have Changed', the blues songs on *"Love And Theft"*, including 'Lonesome Day Blues' and 'High Water (For Charley Patton)', and the folk- and blues-derived songs on *Modern Times*. Many other songs have distinct pentatonic sections, including the verses of 'It Ain't Me, Babe', 'It's Alright, Ma (I'm Only Bleeding)', 'I Threw It All Away', 'Tonight I'll Be Staying Here With You', 'Covenant Woman' and 'Jokerman'. Numerous other songs have a pentatonic feel, even if they are not "purely" pentatonic (and there are rarely pure scales, modes, and notes in popular music anyway).

Pentatonic melodies share characteristics with many other resources in Dylan's sonic palette – they don't appear to go anywhere. Their prevalence in numerous folk styles around the world, their "natural" melodic shape (moving in whole tones or minor thirds, derived from fourths and fifths) and their lack of the modern "leading" (semitone) note are qualities which for Mellers are indicative of certain metaphysical properties:

> Such tunes therefore have little sense of temporality; far from trying to "get somewhere", they live in an existential present, affirming our identity with Nature, even with the Cosmos, cradling us on the bosom of the unconscious deep, winging us into the air. They either induce acceptance – of "fate", of what life does *to* us – or offer some kind of religious subli- mation; what they do not do is to attempt to boss Nature or to assert one person's will at the expense of others. (1981: 144)

Many of Dylan's songs can give the impression of being suspended in a permanent now. In 'Not Dark Yet', a song with an almost entirely pentatonic melody, this is explicit in the lyrics when Dylan sings "I know it looks like I'm moving, but I'm standing still". Dylan's songs can take us on a never- ending cyclical journey, returning again and again to the point we thought we'd just left, inducing an experience of the present at one remove from linear clock time; this is a characteristic they share with much folk, devotional and mystically inclined music that uses pentatonic melodies. In contrast, Dylan's more assertive songs (such as 'Like A Rolling Stone') tend to be diatonic. In general, Dylan's songs are distinct from much popular music, a marked contrast to those songwriters who quite deliberately construct their songs to develop, to progress, to go somewhere – whether this is attempted through modulation (a change of key) or a developmental structure (the addition of new elements to the song).

'All Along The Watchtower' has a pentatonic melody sung with a basic strophic song structure: the repeated chord sequence of C# minor, B, A (on *John Wesley Harding*), or A minor, G, F (for most concerts during the 1970s), or B minor, A, G (for much of the 1980s and 2000s). The strophic structure, the use of riffs, the pentatonic melody, and verses that can be delivered in any sequence allow the song to last for as long as Dylan wishes. The song form and structure contain no logical point of resolution or conclusion; this has to be realized in performance (and it is difficult to fade out as if it were a recording). In earlier years, the final line, "the wind began to howl", would often be followed by sonic stylization of howling winds on the harmonica or guitar before the band was eventually brought to a halt after some extended riffing. In later years, particularly in 2005 through 2007, when the song became the final number in the set, 'All Along The Watchtower' would be brought to a close by Dylan concluding the vocal on the eighth line as initially recorded – "none of them along the line know what any of it is worth" – and the musicians then hitting a final conclusive (even corny), defiant ringing B major chord (rather than the anticipated minor) to end the song and close the concert. (As an aside, Dylan's concerts have usually ended in an upbeat manner; his albums have often ended with a more reflexive, introspective song.)

The magic of the chant and minor third

Many of Bob Dylan's songs use a chant, in Richard Middleton's (1990) terms, or an incantation, in Wilfred Mellers's (1984) terms. Chants catch the moment where speech meets singing, using repetition, emphasizing rhythm and tending towards one pitch. The verses of two of his greatest songs are largely chants: 'It's Alright, Ma (I'm Only Bleeding)' is more or less chanted on one note with occasional shifts up a minor third; many of the verses of 'Like A Rolling Stone' are also chanted on the note C (over a rising chord sequence common to many songs of the late 1950s and early 1960s).

Chanting is integral to human cultures from work songs and children's games to secular festivities and sacred rituals. The chant unites us in the playground; the chant helps us get the job done; the chant helps our team score the winning goal; the chant helps us get closer to our god; the chant unites us at a political rally or demonstration; the chant allows us to celebrate all manner of events in our lives. Yet, the significance of the chant has been ignored or dismissed, for the same reason that scholars look down on apparently "simple" melodies. This is what Bowden writes about 'A Hard Rain's A-Gonna Fall':

> The entire song is one of Dylan's more monotonous. Its melody is almost a chant: the vocal range is less than an octave, and only in the penultimate line of each stanza do notes occur more than a third apart. (2001: 14)

Technically, the tune may be literally "monotonous". But why should the narrow vocal range be singled out for criticism? As for the third, this is a significant little musical interval, particularly the minor third.

The minor third interval (a distance separating pitches of a tone and a half, in contrast to the gap of two whole tones that characterizes the major third) crops up again and again in Dylan's melodies, as it does in much popular music. According to the *New Grove Dictionary of Music and Musicians*, the descending minor third is a "universal manifestation of the melodic impulse" and a characteristic of children's singsongs around the world (Ringer 2001: 363). For those unfamiliar with musical terminology, the opening two notes of the vocal melody of 'Hey Jude' descend over the interval of a minor third, as does the Oasis song 'Live Forever', and when children make fun of each other their mocking singsong ("nah-nah, nah-nah") is based on the minor third. The minor third can also be heard in the intonation of speaking. A notable example is when Dylan addresses "señor", in the song of this name (on *Street Legal*), using the word for the second time with a questioning rising minor third before asking, "Can you tell me where we're heading?" As Van der Merwe has remarked:

> One of the great puzzles of music is the mysteriously satisfying quality of the minor third ... Why should such an awkward interval like the minor third ... come so readily to the human voice? Why should it have the air of what can only be called solidity? The primeval chant consisting ... of nothing but a falling minor third appears in places as different as the Catholic liturgy and the school playground. (1989: 121)

The melody of 'Subterranean Homesick Blues' combines the chant and the minor third. It is mostly sung on one pitch, the note C (a flattened "blue" third in A), with occasional drops down to the minor third below (A), every time Dylan sings "look out kid". The influences on 'Subterranean Homesick Blues' are quite easy to detect and have been acknowledged by Dylan over the years. As he once said, "It's from Chuck Berry ... A bit of 'Too Much Monkey Business' and some of the scat singers of the '40s" (Hilburn 2005: 74). It is certainly possible to hear the influence of Louis Jordan's scat, acknowledged as an influence by both Berry and Dylan. Others have detected 'Taking It Easy', written by Woody Guthrie and Pete Seeger (using the pseudonym of Paul Campbell). Inspired by Berry's dissatisfaction with schooling, menial jobs, domesticity and respectability, 'Subterranean Homesick Blues' is a list of caustic observations about the impact of institutions, authority and respectability. It has been described as a blend of beat poetry and rhythm and blues.

In the last chapter I quoted Ricks referring to the "Skeltonic raids" that produced 'Subterranean Homesick Blues'. The same stance is adopted by Mike Marqusee, who links the song to the "'rude railings' of the ... sixteenth-century English poet John Skelton ... Although he was certainly unaware of it, Dylan makes frequent use of 'Skeltonics' – short, irregular lines in which rhyme is the only fixed principle" (2003: 136). This is yet another example of the appropriation of Dylan for a high-culture agenda and a literary tradition to which he doesn't really belong (and which the writer even presumes him to be "unaware of").

Marqusee also boldly claims that the song is "an obvious forerunner of hip-hop" (*ibid.*). This is an assertion that has been made with tedious regularity when Dylan scholars have focused on their man isolated from the surrounding music culture. Heylin writes that 'Subterranean Homesick Blues' "presaged the advent of rap" (2000: 181); Williams writes that "Subterranean Homesick Blues ... can be heard as a brilliant early example of rap music" (1990: 126); Nigel Williamson writes that "'Subterranean Homesick Blues' can lay claim to be the world's first prototype rap song" (2004: 156). To make such a claim is to completely misrepresent and to undermine the specific historical tradition from which hip-hop and rap have emerged, and to accord Dylan an influence that is completely unwarranted, particularly when allied to an assertion that the song's lineage is European literary

Skeltonics and not African-American scat, blues and r'n'b (styles that quite clearly fed rap). 'Subterranean Homesick Blues' is more derivative than innovative. Not a lesser song, but another example of Dylan as imitator rather than instigator. In turn, Elvis Costello's 'Pump It Up', REM's 'It's The End Of The World As We Know It' and Stephen Still's 'Seen Enough' owe a debt to 'Subterranean Homesick Blues' and continue the musical lineage.

Bob Dylan's music is loaded with riffs, strophic cycles, blues sequences, shout-and-fall patterns, pentatonic melodies, minor thirds and chants – all heavily indebted to blues, folk, gospel and country. It is music that takes the pleasures of repetition, of circularity, of the recurring familiar tune, of apparent stasis, and integrates them with that characteristic Dylanesque poetics and rhyme, delivered with his idiosyncratic and intense range of voices.

Dylan's rhythms

The riff, the rhyme and the chant gain much of their power from rhythm as much as repeated, cyclical melodies. Chanting emphasizes the pulse or beat, the rhythmic melody, the sound of the word with the beat. Chants are popular, in life as much as in music, because we tend to enter melody through the rhythm. When children learn songs, they tend to beat out the rhythmic pattern of the instrumental or vocal melody first. They then work out the other rhythms and pulses in the music. Only after all this do they learn the pitch changes that make up the melody. Lucy Green (2005) discovered this when she researched the way schoolchildren learn to play songs together among friends. When children learn to play music by listening, they intuitively respond to the rhythms of the melodies. Regardless of genre, they beat out the rhythm of the main instrumental or vocal melodies before working out the pitches of these melodies. Green suggested that this might be a stage that people go through as they acquire musical skills and start to recognize pitches. It implies that when people respond to music they are reacting to the movement or flow (the pulse or beat) as much as to the pitch contours of the melody (and this occurs way before they figure out the lyrics).

In classical music, value is accorded to the pitch of the melody and harmony over and above rhythm. This is not the case in most popular music, particularly that derived from blues and folk. In Dylan's music the melodies are integrally tied up with rhythms. That's how we experience them as listeners and that's how the audience enters and becomes part of these songs. The pitches of Dylan's melodies are played out and off against the rhythms of his vocal delivery, and with the rhythms of instruments. Williams heard this characteristic when listening to Dylan's early songs, performed on acoustic guitar in the 1960s, observing that "a primary aspect of his songwriting and performance is a kind of percussive lyricism, as if every word were a pulse in a rhythmic flow" (1990: 69).

Dylan has acquired this percussive lyricism, using words as a pulse in a rhythmic flow, from his immersion in the blues. Jeff Todd Titon highlights this quality when discussing blues singers, particularly Charley Patton, who "was able to give a sequence of dynamic accents to a vowel sound held through successive pitches, lending a percussive rhythmic effect which could – and did – contrast with the rhythm of his guitar accompaniment" (1994: 144). Patton, along with Robert Johnson, was a big influence on Dylan, not only musically and lyrically but also in terms of how they used rhythms.

All Delta blues players used rhythmic irregularities when performing. According to Charles Ford's detailed analysis, Charley Patton used five- and seven-beat bars fairly systematically at the end of four-bar sections, whereas Skip James seemed to perform "with no concern for hypermetre, metre or even beat" (Ford 1998: 71). Ford characterizes Robert Johnson as "systematically irregular", and sets himself the task of going through Johnson's available recordings and trying to work out how many bars are contained within specific sequences, calculating the number of beats in bars and estimating where the bar lines fall. It is not easy, and in frustration Ford remarks "sometimes Robert Johnson's rhythmic irregularities are ambiguous, if not downright indecipherable" (*ibid.*: 80). When he attempts to analyse 'Preaching Blues' he is forced to admit that the song "challenges the validity of my analytic method more obviously than any other" (*ibid.*: 82). After setting out his rhythmic analysis as a sequence of numbers, Ford then adds an even larger caveat: having "spent hundreds of hours ... attempting to measure this music against a constantly, though minutely varying pulse ... I have indeed found the metre highly elusive!" (*ibid.*: 86).

Ford's study of Robert Johnson's rhythms is fascinating. He demonstrates the problems, if not the outright futility, of approaching rhythm through the concepts of bars, beats and regular pulse. He highlights an important quality, found in the music of many great musicians who have adroitly applied rhythmic irregularity when creating a groove or feel.

When playing folk songs Dylan had followed Pete Seeger's advice that singers should avoid predictability when repeating melodic sequences, doing this by holding notes in unexpected places and adding extra beats (see Chapter 3). The combined influence of irregularities absorbed from folk ballads and blues can be heard on recordings when Dylan is playing just acoustic guitar and harmonica, or piano. He will introduce subtle variations in tempo (slowing down, speeding up, seeming to hesitate). He will add beats, drop beats, appear to start a verse or chorus slightly early, and sing verses and choruses in slightly different ways. This is apparent in all his early albums and particularly noticeable throughout *Another Side Of Bob Dylan*, especially on 'My Back Pages', 'Ballad In Plain D' and 'Chimes Of Freedom'. It is a feature that those who attempt covers of Dylan's songs often neglect, so that their versions sound strangely rigid and repressed.

It is harder to hear these irregular inflections when Dylan is performing with a band, as the arrangement and drummer's timing tend to regularize the pulse. Yet the irregularities are often still there. They are noticeable on *Oh Mercy*, particularly on 'Ring Them Bells' and 'What Good Am I?', when Dylan is directing the songs from the piano. Although irregular vocal deliveries are a characteristic of Dylan's songs, he has rarely arranged songs with systematic or structured irregularities. A rare, notable exception is 'We Better Talk This Over' on *Street Legal*, which switches from a regular four-beat pulse to an occasional "bar" with five beats, as if to emphasize the awkwardness of the circumstances evoked in the lyrics (lovers needing to sort out the problems in their relationship).

Although he has given many interviews, Dylan has rarely spoken about rhythm. His most extensive discussion of it can be found in *Chronicles: Volume One*, in a section that a number of people have found baffling, Phil Sutcliffe describing it as "incomprehensible to laymen and opaque to musicians" (2006: 68). This is a passage where Dylan reflects on how his stage performances in the middle of the 1980s had become "habit and routine" characterized by "a casual Carter Family flat-picking style". Thinking about how he might reorient his guitar-playing on stage, he recalled advice given to him by the jazz and blues musician Lonnie Johnson back in 1962. Johnson had demonstrated an approach that Dylan remembered as "a style of playing based on an odd- instead of an even-number system". Here is an extended (but edited) extract:

> It's a highly controlled system of playing and relates to the notes of the scale, how they combine numerically, how they form melodies out of triplets and are axiomatic to the rhythm and chord changes ... The method works on higher or lower degrees depending on different patterns and the syncopation of the piece ... The system works in a cyclical way. Because you're thinking in odd numbers instead of even numbers, you're playing with a different value system. Popular music is usually based on the number 2 and then filled in with fabrics, colors, effects and technical wizardry to make a point. But the total effect is usually depressing and oppressive ... if you are using an odd numerical system, things that strengthen a performance begin to happen and make it memorable for the ages. You don't have to plan or think ahead. In a diatonic scale there are eight notes, in a pentatonic scale there are five. If you're using the first scale, and you hit 2, 5 and 7 to the phrase and then repeat it, a melody forms. Or you can use 2 three times. Or you can use 4 once and 7 twice. It's infinite what you can do, and each time would create a different melody. The possibilities are endless. A song executes itself on several fronts and you can ignore musical customs. All you need is a drummer and a bass player, and all shortcomings become irrelevant as long as you stick to the system. With any type of imagination you can hit notes at intervals and between backbeats, creating counterpoint lines and then you sing off of it. There's no mystery to it and it's not a technical trick. (Dylan 2004: 157–8)

Dylan then goes on to write about how it "works on its own mathematical formula", commenting that "the number 3 is more metaphysically powerful than the number 2" and claims it is "a style that benefits the singer. In folk oriented and jazz–blues songs, it's perfect" (*ibid.*: 159). Dylan self-consciously adopted this approach, he says, from the late 1980s to revitalize his playing. He was aware that audiences familiar with his songs "might be a little confounded by the way they now were about to be played" but he was determined that the songs would be driven by the way "triplet forms would fashion melodies at intervals" (*ibid.*: 160), rather than the existing lyrical content.

There are many things to say about this, and I shall restrict myself to four points. First, a thought that has probably crossed the minds of many people: is Dylan putting us on? Within the context of the memoirs as a whole, I think this is unlikely. The fact that he takes considerable space to discuss this shows just how important it was to his music at this moment. It appears to be a genuine attempt to convey the system that started guiding his live performances. Second, Dylan is not explaining this as a schooled music theorist, nor as a musician trained in the terminology of art music. He's explaining it from the experience of a self-taught musician. It is hard enough to convey these ideas with any clarity, whatever vocabulary you choose to use. So, it should not be judged according to formal music theory. Third, it seems fair to assume that like any "system" it works as a guiding principle, not as a set of rigid rules. When Dylan uses the pentatonic (five-note) scale for melodies, it doesn't mean that every single note of a song can be plotted according to just these five notes. Fourth, the explanation is an attempt to convey the quite conscious way that rhythm allowed him to rethink how he formed melodies, delivered words and combined rhythm, melody and chords. The triplet was the catalyst that allowed him to change the approach to how he rearranged and performed songs in concert. It freed him up to rethink rhythmic patterns and the way syncopation might intersect with and be implicated in the melody of a song (and vice versa). Forming melodies out of the numbered notes of the scale and creating rhythms out of pulses of two and three are linked. It is an idea and an impulse he feels when he plays (again, quite regardless of whether it corresponds with formal music theory).

Dylan adds a degree of clarity with an example: "Link Wray had done the same thing in his classic song 'Rumble' ... Link's song had no lyrics, but he played with the same numerical system" (*ibid.*: 160). Dylan opened some of his shows at Brixton Academy in London with 'Rumble' just after Link Wray died in November 2005. Wray's track can be heard in 4/4 time but with triplets, making it more like a 12/8 blues, with a descending guitar line of accented triplets at the end of each sequence. Similar triplet patterns can be heard in a lot of his songs, and much popular music has drawn from the way folk and blues integrate faster pulses of three with or against a slower pulse of two, creating an overall swinging or rocking motion (it can be heard on 'A Hard Rain's A-Gonna Fall' or 'Isis' or 'Man In The Long Black Coat').

It was from the late 1980s, with the Never Ending Tour, that Dylan began to self-consciously experiment with the vertical and horizontal axis of his songs (rather than the textures of his bands). With the flutes, saxophones, keyboards, and gospel vocals dispensed with in favour of bass, guitar and drums, the arrangement of Dylan's songs in performances began to display a greater interest in the vertical layering of rhythm and melody against each other, and the horizontal way in which the melody and rhythm unfold and enfold each other in time. This can be heard if you think of Dylan's songs in performance as composed of rhythms and, in your mind, you try to factor out the pitch of the melodies and the meaning of the words. Listen to the rhythm of the vocal line, the way the words are rhythmically delivered, along with the rhythms of the guitar, the rhythms of the harmonica. It is not easy, and it may not provide "evidence" of his "system", but it gives a pretty clear indication of how he uses rhythm and melody in his arrangements.

One specific song that Dylan has discussed in terms of its rhythms is 'Cold Irons Bound', which first appeared on *Time Out Of Mind* in 1997. The song is imbued with desperation for a love that has died. The narrator is either bound in cold irons (chains) or bound for a destination called Cold Irons. Dylan has spoken of the initial recording made with Daniel Lanois in these terms:

> "Yeh, there's a real drive to it, but it isn't close to the way I had envisioned ... there were things I had to throw out because this assortment of people just couldn't lock in on riffs and rhythms all together ... I feel there was sameness to the rhythms. It was more like that swampy, voodoo thing that Lanois is so good at. I just wish I'd been able to get more of a legitimate rhythm-oriented sense into it. I didn't feel there was any mathematical thing about that record at all. The one beat could've been anywhere, when instead, the singer should have been defining where the drum should be." (Muir 2003: 251)

There are many rhythms running through this recording, most obviously a recurrent beat of "three, three, two" over or within a more regular rock pulse of 4/4. It is not difficult to sympathize with Dylan's reservations about the "swampy" production with too much going on. He re-recorded the song for the film *Masked and Anonymous* (released on the soundtrack album in 2003). On this version the drums are playing far more directly to, and off against, the vocal line.

By the summer of 2006, 'Cold Irons Bound' had been rearranged again, the rhythm punchier, sparser, yet more direct and more obviously a blues. Seeing Dylan in Bournemouth at this time I was struck by his position at the keyboard on stage and the way he made constant eye contact with the drummer, George Receli. This was pronounced during 'Like A Rolling Stone', when Dylan constantly looked towards Receli as he sang. An interplay developed with the rhythm of the lyrics being played off and to the tom-tom and snare drum. As the song built, Dylan began splitting and spitting the lyrics in a stabbing staccato "you're in – vi – si – ble you've got no se – crets to con – ceal", the rhythm of the vocals driving the song forward. It was a vivid example of what Dylan meant by "the singer defining where the drum should be".

This was also an example of Dylan directing the band during the realization of a specific arrangement of the song, something that he has done more noticeably since playing keyboards on stage. Throughout the NET, Dylan seems to have found a means of arranging songs in such a way as to avoid the extremes that characterized some of his earlier tours, between the elaborate, tight arrangements of 1978 (initially organized by Rob Stoner), when there would be little change from night to night (the arrangements and size of ensemble restricting the opportunities for variation and spontaneity) and the looseness and outright chaos of some performances during the mid-1980s (when no one seemed to be directing). It has clearly been a gradual process, dependent upon the musicians that Dylan has employed and his apparent willingness to convey his musical ideas to them; there were occasional moments during the early 1990s when the song arrangements would collapse into disorganized chaos. One of the appeals of Dylan's concerts for his fans is the anticipation of the new arrangements that he has continually introduced over the years, particularly when returning to the stage after a short break in touring.

© Harry Scott/Redferns

On stage in London 2007

On one of the few occasions that Dylan has commented on his song arrangements, he told Jonathan Lethem:

> "I've heard it said, you've probably heard it said, that all the arrangements change night after night. Well, *that's* a bunch of bullshit, they don't know what they're talking about. The arrangements don't change night after night. The rhythmic structures are different, that's all. You can't change the arrangement night after night – it's *impossible.*" (2006: 78)

Again, Dylan stresses that it is the "rhythmic structures" that are varied, that are modified and allow for improvisation from night to night. From his earliest recordings and performances, the rhythms of the instruments (even the lone acoustic guitar) have never been simply an "accompaniment" in Dylan's songs. They have been integral to the changing sonic architecture of the songs. And – with all those words to play around with – it has so often been the voice that defines, even dictates, the rhythms of Dylan's music.

Inside the melody and the melody inside

When people dismiss Dylan's melodies as "simple", they are bringing to this description a whole bunch of assumptions about the formal qualities that characterize good melodies, consciously or inadvertently derived from the study and criticism of art music. So far I've argued that this ignores the way melodies work in folk, blues and pop music. I want to end this book by taking one step further and draw on the writings of Gino Stefani (1987), who has argued that the study of popular music should develop an alternative approach to melody, one that is connected to the experiences of listeners. He writes that melody should be treated as

> that dimension of music which everyone can easily appropriate in many ways: with the voice by singing, whistling or putting words to it; with the body by dancing, marching etc ... melody ... is what people appropriate most in music ... there is no doubt that the most prominent feature [is] that it is "singable" ... Oral melody is the voice of pleasure: nature teaches us so from childhood. (1987: 21–3)

From an early age we learn to love what many critics have dismissed as simple, boring and repetitive melodies (whether nursery rhymes, festive chants, devotional tunes or pop songs). This is what makes them aesthetically important in our lives and worth discussing. John Lennon instinctively knew this, which is, perhaps, why he recycled the three-note descending melody of 'Three Blind Mice' in so many of his songs. In his detailed study of the Beatles' music, Mellers called this a "refrain which is so fundamental to John's music" (1976: 176). It can most obviously be heard in the "love, love, love" of 'All You Need Is Love', and in 'Oh Yoko' and 'My Mummy's Dead'. The nursery rhymes that children sing, dance, clap with, often entail chants on one pitch, or short walks up and down the scale, or rising or falling thirds and fourths. So do the songs that people carry with them and sing when working, doing domestic chores, in the shower, on the street, or at a concert.

Bob Dylan's melodies and rhythms do not exist as isolated structures or texts, but as songs that connect with and are embedded into people's lives. This can be illustrated with reference to the song 'It Ain't Me, Babe', first released in 1964. Following an observation made by a newspaper reviewer at the time, many writers have noted that the "No, no, no" refrain of this song, coming out in 1964, can be heard as a response to the "Yeah, yeah, yeah" refrain of the Beatles' 'She Loves You', released the previous year. Bowden is just one writer who has made this point about the two early songs:

> The Beatles had until then sung simple love-song lyrics in adapted gospel style; Dylan, adapting blues style, exactly reversed the sentiments. "She loves you, yeah, yeah, yeah," they sang, and he sang "No, no, no, it ain't me babe". (2001: 104)

Whether or not this was a conscious response, and whether there was any irony intended, there were many ways that Dylan and the Beatles musically commented on each other's work throughout the 1960s. This includes complementary homage (Lennon's 'You've Got To Hide Your Love Away' and 'I'm A Loser'; Dylan's band arrangements on *Bringing It All Back Home*; Harrison's 'Long, Long, Long', with its acoustic guitar and organ texture, and chord sequence with descending bass line borrowed from 'Sad-Eyed Lady Of The Lowlands') and more ironic or sarcastic references (Dylan's '4th Time Around', which comments on 'Norwegian Wood', and McCartney's 'Rocky Raccoon', which pokes fun at the Wild West imagery of *John Wesley Harding*).

Both the Beatles and Dylan sing "yeah, yeah, yeah" / "no, no, no" over three notes descending within the interval of a minor third, and the same notes at that (G, F#, E), but they are quite obviously harmonized differently. The Beatles' melody is more directly related to the underlying chords, while Dylan's is a typical bluesy folk melody that bears only a tenuous "functional" relationship to the chords. Either way, the melodies of the main chorus hook are the same.

In approaching the songs of Dylan and the Beatles, a music analyst may not wish to detach the melody from the chords, rhythms, instrumentation and so on. But, drawing on Stefani's suggestion, we can think of melodies as tunes that are heard, appropriated and sung independently from the chords and harmony, by listeners in their everyday lives, whether or not they are listening to a recording. When they are sung by fans at concerts, performers gain a tangible sense of how their tunes have connected with the public. This can be heard on the performance of 'It Ain't Me, Babe' on the album *Real*

Live, recorded in England and Ireland during the summer of 1984, when Dylan stands back from the microphone and allows the crowd to sing the "No, no, no," refrain (it can also be heard on many bootlegs since that time).

People have been singing along at Bob Dylan concerts since at least the 1974 US tour with the Band. Singing along seemed to gain momentum at Dylan concerts during the middle of the 1980s, particularly from 1984. Williams recounts this episode from Dylan's European tour of that year:

> An Italian television station filmed three and a half songs from the Barcelona (Spain) concert. The footage of the last encore, 'Blowin' In The Wind', is priceless. Dylan had been encouraging the fans to sing along on the choruses to this song for about two weeks, but on this evening the crowd – who had been wonderful all through the performance, despite the fact that it didn't start till after midnight – caught Dylan by surprise. They start singing – loudly and in fine harmony – at the start of the first chorus (no doubt they all saw newspaper or TV coverage of the Madrid concert two days earlier), and Dylan is visibly moved. He sings the next verse in his best "big and earnest" voice, and then choreographs the singalong with a verve that would make Pete Seeger proud. (1992: 259)

Bob Dylan might not be the most obvious musician to sing along with—after all, he is not usually perceived as someone who goes out on stage to entertain and engage in dialogue with a crowd. Yet, in other respects he is heir to the legacies of a type of social, communal music-making that refracts back from contemporary pop and rock through folk and blues, to street-sung broadsides and work songs, to the melodic observations of medieval troubadours and the sacred rhythms of Christianity and Judaism. There are many characteristics common to the rich sonic tradition that I am attempting to signal with these brief words. The most notable is the way melodies in the popular song work at the intersection of speech and singing, the elevated and the mundane; the song starts when talk becomes music, when the ordinary becomes special.

Despite the historical importance of communal singing in folk and popular culture, some writers have taken exception to people singing at Dylan concerts. Andrew Muir endorses comments made by Ian Bell, who had written of Dylan's changing song arrangements and argued that they were "challenging the audience even to attempt to 'sing along' with songs they thought they knew. As a believer in corporal punishment for lachrymose community singing, this writer, for one, owes him a debt" (Bell, cited in Muir 2001: 191). Muir comments "this writer makes it two". It is highly unlikely that Dylan's exploration of his songs in concert is motivated by such a simplistic desire to subvert and undermine audience attempts to sing along. If anything, the new melodies and rhythms are often playing off and held in tension to the previously heard melodies and rhythms, whether it becomes tangible when people try to sing, or whether the audience become aware of it as the song unfolds against their memory of how the song last sounded.

After a concert in Barrowlands, Glasgow, in June 2004, the Expecting Rain website had a number of contributions from people who had been at the gig and who remarked upon the singing and the way Dylan responded to it. According to what was written by audience members, the fans were loudly singing along with 'Just Like A Woman', 'It Ain't Me, Babe' and 'Like A Rolling Stone'. One audience member said Dylan was pointing at the audience and conducting them during 'Like A Rolling Stone'. Then he said (something like, there are minor variations in how four people recount what he said), "We've played that thousands of times and people try to sing along, but nobody can ever do it" or "We've done that song a thousand times and no one's kept up like that". He then mimed the opening lines of 'All Along The Watchtower' while the crowd were singing.

Singing along symbolically and tangibly affirms a relationship between musician and audience. The audience enters the song, participates in it and the artist often stops singing and lets the audience take over. Singing along with choruses is also one of the clearest examples of how the words of pop songs become detached from their semantic significance within the song's lyrical narrative or argument. These are quite clearly not the words read on paper. The "No, no, no, it ain't me, babe" refrain becomes a phrase in itself, appropriated, incorporated into the breath of many singers. It can resonate as a defiant riposte to whomever or whatever is bugging an individual audience member in his or her life at that moment, and, at the same time, it is a celebration of the magic of Dylan's song. During an earlier tour with the band in 1974, Williams heard 'It Ain't Me, Babe' as "a song of not just personal but collective freedom" (1992: 8).

During live performances of 'Like A Rolling Stone' the chorus tends to elicit two responses: some audience members sing the words and melody, others cheer in response to "How does it feel?" In concert, that phrase "How does it feel?" is no longer addressed to a character in the lyrics. Instead, it is transformed, becoming "How does it feel?" in the here and now of the concert. It becomes a multivocal celebration of how it feels to be part of the moment and the history of Dylan singing this song. During Dylan's 1974 tour with the Band, Bowden heard the response to this song – the audience singing "How does it feel?" – as "reinforcing the feeling that each listener is not alone but rather part of a community all of whom know how it feels" (2001: 94). Whilst the idea of the audience sharing in the values of a "rock community" has been thoroughly questioned since the 1970s (see Frith 1983), the song has continued to resonate with a collective spirit at concerts, whatever community is being projected, imagined or desired on any particular night.

There is, paradoxically, something quite profound about the way an apparently simple tune can allow large numbers of people to participate in singing along with that melody, sometimes without being fully aware of the meaning, or without even worrying about whether they are singing the correct words. It is quite possible to sing along with songs (at a concert or to a recording) and be unaware of the full lyrics, or the correct lyrics. You can sing some words and sing the nearest-sounding word to others. And we should not underestimate how people sing along with songs without opening their mouths. It is also possible to sing along – aloud or in the mind – while not necessarily agreeing with the apparent sentiments. The contrast between personal belief and lyric is only a contradiction if you assume that songs communicate via the meaning of the words alone, *and* that participation implies agreement with a song's semantic content. "We" are sharing in the sonics, not the semantics.

Singing a song is one of the most embodied, physical ways of putting ourselves into music. Appropriating melodies, putting our stamp on them, chanting them when we are engaged in routines in our homes, when walking down the street or at a concert is how we enter the songs of Bob Dylan and the music of Dylan becomes part of our lives.

Bibliography

Barker, Derek. "*Confessions of a Yakuza* and the Myth of Plagiarism", in D. Barker (ed.), *Bob Dylan: Anthology Volume 2: 20 Years of Isis*, pp. 307–17. New Malden, Surrey: Chrome Dreams, 2005.

Bauldie, John. Liner notes to *The Bootleg Series, Volumes 1–3*. Sony Music, 1991.

Billig, Michael. *Rock'n'Roll Jews*. Nottingham: Five Leaves, 2000.

Booth, Mark. *The Experience of Songs*. New Haven: Yale University Press, 1981.

Bowden, Betsy. *Performed Literature: Words and Music by Bob Dylan*. Lanham, MD: University Press of America, 2001.

Cartwright, Bert. "The Curse It Is Cast: Dylan, God and the American Dream", *The Telegraph*, No. 46 (1993), 91–128.

Christgau, Robert. "The Year of No Next Big Thing", *Village Voice*, 24 February 1998. at www.robertchristgau.com/xg/pnj/pj97.php, accessed 19 September 2007.

Christgau, Robert. "John Wesley Harding", in Benjamin Hedin (ed.), *Studio A: The Bob Dylan Reader*, pp. 64–7. New York: W. W. Norton, 2004.

Clancy, Liam. "Bob Dylan, by Liam Clancy", in Michael Gray and John Bauldie (eds), *All Across the Telegraph: A Bob Dylan Handbook*, pp. 20–2. London: Futura, 1987.

Crowe, Cameron. Liner notes to *Biograph*. Sony Columbia, 1985.

Darden, Robert. *People Get Ready! A New History of Black Gospel Music*. London: Continuum, 2004.

Day, Aidan. *Jokerman: Reading the Lyrics of Bob Dylan*. Oxford: Blackwell, 1988.

DeNora, Tia. *Music in Everyday Life*. Cambridge: Cambridge University Press, 2000.

Doyle, Peter. "From 'My Blue Heaven' to 'Race With The Devil': Echo, Reverb and (Dis)ordered Space in Early Popular Music Recording", *Popular Music*, Vol. 23, No. 1 (2004), 31–50.

Dylan, Bob. *Chronicles: Volume One*. New York: Simon & Schuster, 2004.

Flanagan, Bill. *Written in My Soul: Conversations with Rock's Great Songwriters*. New York: Contemporary Books, 1987.

Ford, Charles. "Robert Johnson's Rhythms", *Popular Music*, Vol. 17, No. 1 (1998), 71–93.

Frith, Simon. *Sound Effects: Youth, Leisure and the Politics of Rock'n'Roll*. Constable: London, 1983.

Frith, Simon. *Performing Rites: On the Value of Popular Music*. Oxford: Oxford University Press, 1996.

Garman, Bryan. *A Race of Singers: Whitman's Working-class Hero from Guthrie to Springsteen*. Chapel Hill, NC: University of North Carolina Press, 2000.

Gill, Andy and Odegard, Kevin. *A Simple Twist of Fate: Bob Dylan and the Making of Blood On The Tracks*. New York: Da Capo, 2004.

Gilmour, Michael. *Tangled Up in the Bible: Bob Dylan and Scripture*. London: Continuum, 2004.

Ginsberg, Allen. "Songs of Redemption", in liner notes to *Desire*, pp.19–22. Sony Music, 1976.

Godu, Teresa. "Bloody Daggers and Lonesome Graveyards: The Gothic and Country Music", in Cecelia Tichi (ed.), *Readin' Country Music: Steel Guitars, Opry Stars and Honky Tonk Bars*, pp. 57–80. Durham, NC: Duke University Press, 1995.

Gray, Michael. *Song and Dance Man III: The Art of Bob Dylan*. London: Continuum, 2000.

Gray, Michael. *The Bob Dylan Encyclopedia*. London: Continuum, 2006.

Green, Lucy. "Meaning, Autonomy and Authenticity in the Music Classroom", Inaugural Lecture, Institute of Education, London. 7 December 2005.

Griffiths, Dai. "From Lyric to Anti-lyric: Analyzing the Words in Pop Song", in Allan Moore (ed.), *Analyzing Popular Music*. Cambridge: Cambridge University Press, 2003.

Guralnick, Peter. *Searching for Robert Johnson*. New York: Plume, 1989.

Hajdu, David. *Positively Fourth Street: The Lives and Times of Joan Baez, Bob Dylan, Mimi Fariña and Richard Fariña*. Bloomsbury: London, 2002.

Hammond, John, with Irving Townshend. *John Hammond on Record*. New York: Ridge Press, 1977.

Heylin, Clinton. *Bob Dylan: Behind the Shades. Take Two*. Harmondsworth: Penguin, 2000.

Hilburn, Robert. "When I Paint My Masterpiece", *Mojo*, No. 142 (2005), 72–4.

Hinchey, John. "Stealing Home: Bob Dylan Then and Now", *The Telegraph*, No. 32 (1989), 43–59.

Laing, Dave. "*31 Songs* and Nick Hornby's Pop Ideology", *Popular Music*, Vol. 24, No. 2 (2005), 269–72.

Lethem, Jonathan. "The Genius of Bob Dylan", *Rolling Stone*, 7 September 2006, 75–100.

Lindley, John. "Movies Inside His Head. *Empire Burlesque* and *The Maltese Falcon*", *The Telegraph*, No 25 (1986), 75–80.

Lipsitz, George. *Time Passages: Collective Memory and American Popular Culture*. Minneapolis: University of Minnesota Press, 1990.

Marcus, Greil. *Mystery Train*. New York: Omnibus Press, 1977.

Marcus, Greil. *Invisible Republic: Bob Dylan's Basement Tapes*. New York: Henry Holt, 1997.

Marcus, Greil. *Like A Rolling Stone: Bob Dylan at the Crossroads*. Boulder, CO: Public Affairs, 2005.

Marqusee, Mike. *Chimes of Freedom: The Politics of Bob Dylan's Art*. New York: The New Press, 2003.

Marshall, Lee. *Bob Dylan: The Never Ending Star*. Cambridge: Polity Press, 2007.

Mellers, Wilfred. *Twilight of the Gods: The Beatles in Retrospect*. London: Faber and Faber, 1976.

Mellers, Wilfrid. "God, Modality and Meaning in Some Recent Songs of Bob Dylan", *Popular Music*, Vol. 1 (1981), 143–57.

Mellers, Wilfred. *A Darker Shade of Pale: A Backdrop to Bob Dylan*. Oxford: Oxford University Press, 1984.

Middleton, Richard. *Studying Popular Music*. Milton Keynes: Open University Press, 1990.

Miles, Barry. *Ginsberg: A Biography*. London: Viking, 1990.

Muir, Andrew. *Razor's Edge: Bob Dylan and the Never Ending Tour*. London: Helter Skelter, 2001.

Muir, Andrew. *Troubadour: Early & Late Songs of Bob Dylan*. Huntingdon: Woodstock Books, 2003.

Murray, Albert. *Stomping the Blues*. New York: Da Capo, 2000 [first published 1976].

Oliver, Paul. *Blues Fell This Morning: Meaning in the Blues*. Cambridge: Cambridge University Press, 1990.

Opie, Iona, and Opie, Peter. *The Oxford Dictionary of Nursery Rhymes*. Oxford: Oxford University Press, 1997 [first published 1951].

Pareles, Jon. "A Wiser Voice Blowin' in the Autumn Wind", *New York Times*, 27 September 1997.

Peterson, Richard. *Creating Country Music: Fabricating Authenticity.* Chicago: University of Chicago Press, 1997.

Polizzotti, Mark. *Highway 61 Revisited.* London: Continuum, 2006.

Quinn, Anthony. "It Ain't Me, Babe", *Daily Telegraph (Books)*, 13 September 2003, p. 3.

Ricks, Christopher. *Dylan's Visions of Sin.* London: Viking, 2003.

Ringer, Alexander. "Melody", in Stanley Sadie (ed.), *The New Grove Dictionary of Music and Musicians*, Vol. 16, pp. 363–73. London: Macmillan, 2001.

Roe, Nicholas. "Playing Time", in Neil Corcoran (ed.), *'Do You, Mr Jones?': Bob Dylan with the Poets and Professors*, pp. 81–104. London: Pimlico, 2003.

Rosenbaum, Ron. "Playboy Interview: Bob Dylan, a Candid Conversation with the Visionary Whose Songs Changed the Times", *Playboy*, March 1978, pp. 61–90.

Ross, Alex. "The Wanderer", in Benjamin Heder (ed.), *Studio A: The Bob Dylan Reader*, pp. 291–312. New York: W. W. Norton, 2004.

Rowland, Marc. Interview with Bob Dylan, Rochester, New York, 23 September 1978. Unpublished.

Schafer, R. Murray. *The Soundscape: Our Sonic Environment and the Tuning of the World.* Rochester, VT: Destiny Books, 1994.

Schuller, Gunther. *Early Jazz: Its Roots and Musical Development.* Oxford: Oxford University Press, 1968.

Scobie, Stephen. *Alias Bob Dylan Revisited.* Calgary: Red Deer Press, 2003.

Shelton, Robert. *No Direction Home: The Life and Music of Bob Dylan.* London: Hodder and Stoughton, 1986. [Paperback editions, New York: Da Capo Press, 1997; Harmondsworth: Penguin, 1987].

Smith, Larry. *Writing Bob Dylan: The Songs of a Lonesome Traveler.* Westport, CT: Praeger, 2005.

Sounes, Howard. *Down the Highway: The Life of Bob Dylan.* London: Black Swan, 2001.

Springs, Helena. "Helena Springs, a Conversation with Chris Cooper", *The Telegraph*, No. 34 (1989), 71–3.

Stefani, Gino. "Melody: A Popular Perspective", *Popular Music*, Vol. 6, No. 1 (1987), 21–35.

Sutcliffe, Phil. "The Comeback Kid", *Mojo*, September 2006, pp. 66–75.

Taft, Michael. *Blues Lyric Poetry: An Anthology.* New York: Garland, 1983.

Tagg, Philip. "Subjectivity and Soundscape, Motorbikes and Music" in H. Järviluoma (ed.), *Soundscapes: Essays on Vroom and Moo*. University of Tampere, Finland, Department of Folk Tradition, 1994.

Tichi, Cecelia. "Country Music Seriously: An Interview with Bill C. Malone", in Cecelia Tichi (ed.), *Readin' Country Music: Steel Guitars, Opry Stars and Honky Tonk Bars*, pp. 341–59. Durham, NC: Duke University Press, 1995.

Titon, Jeff Todd. *Early Downhome Blues*, 2nd edn. Chapel Hill: University of North Carolina Press, 1994.

Trager, Oliver. *Keys to the Rain: The Definitive Bob Dylan Encyclopedia*. New York: Billboard Books, 2004.

Van der Merwe, Peter. *Origins of the Popular Style: Antecedents of Twentieth-century Popular Music*. Oxford: Oxford University Press, 1989.

Van der Merwe, Peter. *Roots of the Classical: The Popular Origins of Western Music*. Oxford: Oxford University Press, 2004.

Van Leeuwen, Theo. *Speech, Music, Sound*. Basingstoke: Macmillan, 1999.

Van Ronk, Dave. *The Mayor of MacDougal Street: A Memoir*. New York: Da Capo Press, 2006.

Weisethaunet, Hans. "Is There Such a Thing as the 'Blue Note'?" *Popular Music*, Vol. 20, No. 1 (2001), 99–116.

Whaley, Preston. *Blows Like a Horn: Beat Writing, Jazz, Style, and Markets in the Transformation of U.S. Culture*. Cambridge, MA: Harvard University Press, 2004.

Williams, Paul. *Bob Dylan, Performing Artist: 1960–1973*. London: Xanadu, 1990.

Williams, Paul. *Bob Dylan, Performing Artist: 1974–1986, The Middle Years*. London: Omnibus Press, 1992.

Williams, Paul. *Bob Dylan, Performing Artist: 1986–1990 and Beyond (Mind Out of Time)*. London: Omnibus Press, 2004.

Williamson, Nigel. *The Rough Guide to Bob Dylan*. London: Rough Guides, 2004.

Zollo, Paul. *Songwriters on Songwriting*, 4th edn. New York: Da Capo, 2003.

Album Discography

These are US issue dates except where otherwise indicated.

Bob Dylan (1962)
The Freewheelin' Bob Dylan (1963)
The Times They Are A-Changin' (1964)
Another Side Of Bob Dylan (1964)
Bringing It All Back Home (1965)
Highway 61 Revisited (1965)
Blonde On Blonde (1966)
Bob Dylan's Greatest Hits (1967)
John Wesley Harding (1967)
Nashville Skyline (1969)
Self Portrait (1970)
New Morning (1970)
Bob Dylan's Greatest Hits Vol. II (1971) [UK title: *More Bob Dylan's Greatest Hits*]
Pat Garrett & Billy The Kid (1973)
Dylan (1973)
Planet Waves (1974)
Before The Flood (1974)
Blood On The Tracks (1975)
The Basement Tapes (1975)
Desire (1976)
Hard Rain (1976)
Street Legal (1978)
Bob Dylan At Budokan (1978)
Slow Train Coming (1979)
Saved (1980)
Shot Of Love (1981)
Infidels (1983)
Real Live (1984)

Empire Burlesque (1985)
Biograph (1985)
Knocked Out Loaded (1986)
Down In The Groove (1988)
Dylan & The Dead (1989)
Oh Mercy (1989)
Under The Red Sky (1990)
The Bootleg Series Volume 1–3 (Rare & Unreleased 1961–1991)
Good As I Been To You (1992)
The 30th Anniversary Concert Celebration (1993)
World Gone Wrong (1993)
Greatest Hits Volume 3 (1994)
MTV Unplugged (1995)
The Best Of Bob Dylan Vol. 2 (1997)
Time Out Of Mind (1997)
The Bootleg Series Vol. 4. Bob Dylan Live 1966. The "Royal Albert Hall"
  Concert (1998)
The Essential Bob Dylan (2000)
Bob Dylan Live 1961–2000 [2001, Japan]
"Love And Theft" (2001)
The Bootleg Series Vol. 5. Bob Dylan Live 1975. The Rolling Thunder Revue
  (2002)
The Bootleg Series Vol. 6. Bob Dylan Live 1964. Concert At Philharmonic
  Hall (2004)
No Direction Home: The Soundtrack. The Bootleg Series Vol. 7 [film
  soundtrack] (2005)
Modern Times (2006)

Note: This list includes only the main official releases of Bob Dylan albums.
For a list of officially released collaborations, rarities and obscure recordings, see www.searchingforagem.com. For a list of bootleg recordings
currently circulating among collectors, see the Bob Dylan Bootleg
Museum at www.bobsboots.com.

Index

Note: As so much of this book concerns Dylan's performing and songwriting there are no separate entries for these.

164 Index